NEW DIRECTIONS FOR ADULT AND CC

Ralph G. Brockett, *University of Tennessee, Knoxville*
EDITOR-IN-CHIEF

Alan B. Knox, *University of Wisconsin, Madison*
CONSULTING EDITOR

Confronting Controversies in Challenging Times: A Call for Action

Michael W. Galbraith
Temple University

Burton R. Sisco
University of Wyoming

EDITORS

Number 54, Summer 1992

JOSSEY-BASS PUBLISHERS
San Francisco

CONFRONTING CONTROVERSIES IN CHALLENGING TIMES:
A CALL FOR ACTION
Michael W. Galbraith, Burton R. Sisco (eds.)
New Directions for Adult and Continuing Education, no. 54
Ralph G. Brockett, Editor-in-Chief
Alan B. Knox, Consulting Editor

Microfilm copies of issues and articles are available in 16mm and 35mm,
as well as microfiche in 105mm, through University Microfilms Inc., 300
North Zeeb Road, Ann Arbor, Michigan 48106.

LC 85-644750   ISSN 0195-2242   ISBN 1-55542-748-0

NEW DIRECTIONS FOR ADULT AND CONTINUING EDUCATION is part of The
Jossey-Bass Higher and Adult Education Series and is published quarterly
by Jossey-Bass Inc., Publishers, 350 Sansome Street, San Francisco, California 94104-1310 (publication number USPS 493-930). Second-class post-
age paid at San Francisco, California, and at additional mailing offices.
POSTMASTER: Send address changes to New Directions for Adult and Continuing Education, Jossey-Bass Inc., Publishers, 350 Sansome Street, San
Francisco, California 94104-1310.

SUBSCRIPTIONS for 1992 cost $45.00 for individuals and $60.00 for institutions, agencies, and libraries.

EDITORIAL CORRESPONDENCE should be sent to the Editor-in-Chief,
Ralph G. Brockett, Dept. of Technological and Adult Education, University
of Tennessee, 402 Claxton Addition, Knoxville, Tennessee 37996-3400.

Cover photograph by Wernher Krutein/PHOTOVAULT © 1990.

 The paper used in this journal is acid-free and meets the strictest
guidelines in the United States for recycled paper (50 percent
recycled waste, including 10 percent postconsumer waste). Manu-
factured in the United States of America.

CONTENTS

EDITORS' NOTES

Most any profession and associated practice is marked by certain controversies or vexing issues. This is true not only of well-established professions such as medicine but also of developing professions such as adult and continuing education. Today, as never before, adult and continuing educators are having to deal with a panoply of issues that impact both the knowledge base and professional practice of the discipline. This volume, *Confronting Controversies in Challenging Times: A Call for Action,* presents a variety of perspectives on some of the more enduring controversies of our times so as to encourage improved practice in adult and continuing education.

In the following chapters, seventeen professional adult and continuing educators present their views on a number of controversies confronting the field today. As a means of guiding the development and writing of each chapter, authors were asked to address the following questions: "What is your position on the controversy? How have you arrived at this position and viewpoint? Has your position changed over time? What literature supports or strengthens your position? And how will your position and/or viewpoint improve the practice of adult and continuing education?"

In Chapter One, we introduce the various controversies presented in this volume and describe three positive consequences that practitioners may derive from taking positions on a controversy. A model for understanding controversies in adult and continuing education is also presented with brief illustrations of how it can be used to improve practice.

The starting point of adult and continuing education has long been an issue in the field. In Chapter Two, Paulette T. Beatty argues that individual change constitutes not only the necessary and sufficient beginning and ending points for adult education but also the focal point for any educational undertaking. In Chapter Three, Paul J. Ilsley takes a different position, arguing that practitioners in adult education should openly accept their primary role as agents for social change.

The issue of professionalization in adult and continuing education has also been hotly debated for some time now. In Chapter Four, Michael Collins offers a number of compelling reasons as to why the field should resist further professionalization. He believes that ambitions toward further professionalization of adult and continuing education are both pretentious and dysfunctional. Ronald M. Cervero, in Chapter Five, disagrees with this position, pointing out that the question of professionalization is nearly a nonissue. He contends that adult educators will continue their efforts toward professionalization and that this is a positive trend.

For many years, professional adult and continuing educators have come from many different disciplines such as sociology, history, political science, and psychology. This diversity is understandable since the field of adult and continuing education is relatively young and an emerging discipline. Today, however, as the knowledge base expands almost exponentially each year, the issue of where leaders in adult and continuing education should come from is receiving more attention. In Chapter Six, Peter Jarvis argues that the leaders should come from outside the field since they will bring different perspectives and understandings that can enrich policy and practice. William S. Griffith, in Chapter Seven, counterargues that leaders who come from outside the field will perpetuate dependence on the clientele, media, and content of their respective disciplines. Adult and continuing education is marked by a robust diversity that can only be advanced by leaders whose training and experience reflect such values and practices. Thus, Griffith argues that leaders must be developed from within the profession.

Whether adult and continuing education should be market driven is another vexing issue facing the field. In Chapter Eight, Hal Beder takes the view that adult and continuing education should not be market driven. He bases this position on three points: market-driven delivery systems are inherently unequal; they maximize the benefits for the educationally, socially, and economically advantaged while minimizing the benefits to the disadvantaged; and they are inefficient systems for meeting critical social needs. Robert C. Mason, in Chapter Nine, counterargues that adult and continuing education must be market driven to survive and suggests that this system helps ensure that client needs are met.

Another issue that has garnered substantial debate over the years is whether continuing education should be mandatory. Ralph G. Brockett, in Chapter Ten, questions the need for mandatory continuing education. He rightfully acknowledges the seductive nature of the issue, noting that many see the mandatory element as a means of protecting consumers from abuse. But Brockett suggests that practitioners and the general public should not be lulled into such false security, since mandatory continuing education does not ensure effective and competent performance. In Chapter Eleven, Barbara F. LeGrand takes the opposite view noting that mandatory continuing education is necessary and is here to stay. She believes that the positive benefits of mandatory continuing education far outweigh any negative consequences and exhorts the profession to take an active role in shaping future efforts in this area.

The issue of a code of ethics for adult and continuing education continues to receive substantial scrutiny in the field. In Chapter Twelve, Phyllis M. Cunningham presents the view that a code of ethics is inappropriate because it helps those individuals who are either in or working toward positions of power. In addition, a code of ethics inhibits the ability of individuals or groups to reconstruct social reality and thereby change the status quo. Thomas J. Sork and Brenda A. Welock, in Chapter Thirteen, present a number of convincing arguments in favor of an ethical code, noting that there are both unwarranted fears and mistaken notions of what constitutes a code of ethics.

Finally, whether adult and continuing education professionals should be certified has been debated for some time. In Chapter Fourteen, Waynne Blue James maintains that because the field is so diverse, it is impossible to develop a certification system for all of the constituents who consider themselves adult and continuing educators. Barbara A. White takes the opposite position in Chapter Fifteen. She argues in favor of certification, believing that it is one way of ensuring professional competence.

In the final chapter, we suggest a set of intellectual standards that can be used by adult and continuing educators in the process of confronting controversies. It is our hope that critical and reflective examination of controversies such as those presented in this volume will lead to a more vibrant and meaningful profession.

Michael W. Galbraith
Burton R. Sisco
Editors

MICHAEL W. GALBRAITH is associate professor of adult education and coordinator of graduate studies in adult education at Temple University, Philadelphia.

BURTON R. SISCO is associate professor of adult education and coordinator of the graduate program in adult and postsecondary education at the University of Wyoming, Laramie.

Controversies confronting adult and continuing education can be understood through an examination of a practical model.

A Model for Understanding Controversies in Adult and Continuing Education

Michael W. Galbraith, Burton R. Sisco

What is a controversy? According to *Webster's Ninth Collegiate Dictionary* (1991, p. 285), a controversy is "a discussion marked especially by the expression of opposing views." Those who read the adult and continuing education literature as well as attend professional association meetings will readily recognize that there are many individuals who are quite pugnacious, spending considerable time debating dilemmas, issues, and controversies confronting the field. Nevertheless, the field of adult and continuing education is often mistakenly perceived by many as rather tame. Over a decade ago, Kreitlow (1981, p. xiii) stated that "observers of practice and programs in this field frequently get the impression that adult educators are people who never get involved in disputes." Today, nothing is further from the truth as evidenced by recent conference programs, conference proceedings, journals, monographs, and books. The field and its associated membership has become more thoughtful and more vocal about policy and practice. Multiple voices are heard in the frequent discussions on controversies confronting the field. Recent publications indicate that adult educators are becoming less tolerant of earlier values, purposes, and professional practices in the field. New perspectives are offered and open for debate on such topics as the purpose of the field (Quigley, 1989; Collins, 1991), literacy (Beder, 1991), ethics (Brockett, 1988), continuing professional education (Cervero, 1988), critical thinking (Brookfield, 1987; Mezirow, 1991), reflective practice (Schön, 1987), self-directed learning (Brockett and Hiemstra, 1991; Candy, 1991), culturally diverse populations (Ross-Gordon, Martin, and Briscoe, 1990), sociocultural contexts for adult learning (Merriam and Caffarella, 1991), and instruction (Galbraith, 1990, 1991; Hiemstra and Sisco, 1990). Perhaps the most telling aspect of a maturing field is its capacity to welcome discussion that is laced with opposing views. While this debate has been generally good for the field, the voices of many adult and continuing education practitioners who could offer additional perspectives on controversies have been muted because of limited outlets for expression.

Many controversies exist in the field of adult and continuing education these days, begging for a forum, a stage, an arena where critical and reflective discourse can take place. Either the location does not exist, or many in the field have little interest in looking at complicated dilemmas and issues, since these controversies seem to go unheard. We have no public opinion polls to indicate how adult and continuing educators feel about the various controversies or to assess the impact of these controversies on the field. Even if we did, public opinion has little to do with private opinion. How we feel about a controversy is in most cases a private matter, seldom shared with any others but close friends and colleagues. Private opinion allows us to examine issues in a fluid, changeable manner. It even allows us to live with contradictions, where our emotions collide with our principles. And yet little is known about the multitude of controversies confronting the field or how many adult educators share the same thoughts and ideas about a controversy or dilemma.

It would seem that controversies in the field of adult and continuing education are grounded in the private side of our being and then extended into a more public forum. Vroom's (1964) expectancy theory may serve as the foundation for individual beliefs concerning adult education controversies. Expectancy theory states that an individual's behavior is strongly affected by his or her anticipation that one particular action will result in more desirable consequences than will other actions. The theory only describes the process by which an individual is motivated. In this case, the theory is utilized to explain what motivates the adult educator to determine if a position is warranted on a particular adult education controversy. Expectancy theory suggests that three kinds of information are necessary to understand motivation and behavior: (1) The belief that personal effort will result in the attainment of some level of knowledge about a controversy is referred to as an *expectancy belief*. (2) *Instrumentality belief* refers to the belief that attainment of some particular knowledge state about the controversy will affect rewards or practical outcomes. (3) The desire for or aversion to some consequence of behavior is referred to as an *outcome valence*. These consequences may be work related, for example, peer acceptance or rejection, or praise for taking a position. They may also be nonwork related, such as reduced time with spouse and family and increased opportunity for leisure.

These three factors influence a person's motivation toward some course of action. If the adult educator believes that attainment of knowledge about a controversy will result in certain personal gain and value, he or she will be motivated to engage in a particular course of action. If the outcome is seen to have no value to them, they will have no motivation to pursue or engage in the challenging activity of working through a controversy and expressing an accepting or opposing point of view. If one is motivated to engage in a course of action that will hopefully produce resolution of the dilemma, then certain consequences for taking a position will be realized.

Consequences of Taking a Position

We believe that the activities of working through a controversy and arriving at an informed position are valuable. Boggs (1981, p. 2) states that to become a controversy in adult education, "a phenomenon, trend, or practice must be significant to affect present and future practice, and individuals must hold differing views on the best course of action in its regard." Frankena (1974) suggests that an author's reasoned discourse on any issue or controversy should include four kinds of normative statements: (1) a statement about what he or she believes adult educators should or should not do with respect to an issue, (2) a statement of the analyses of the arguments, slogans, concepts, and statements that others have used to express opinions on an issue, (3) a statement concerning the chosen position that is supported by empirical facts, hypotheses about their explanation, experimental findings, and predictions, and (4) a statement describing how to accomplish the desired objectives, providing evidence and arguments to justify the process. Boggs (1981, p. 2) professes that to respond to an issue-oriented discourse, adult educators must be analytical and search for internal consistency "in the beliefs, commitments, and criteria stated by the author"; that is, they have to locate and examine assumptions and meanings of words employed by the author. Second, Boggs suggests that the adult educator must be able to "augment his analysis of the positions and argument of the authors with his own conclusions to guide professional practice" (p. 2). Three positive consequences emerge from the works of Boggs and Frankena with which an adult educator must contend when taking a position on a controversy.

Enhances Critical Thinking. The first consequence of taking a position is engagement in critical thinking. Brookfield (1987, p. 1) states that critical thinking "involves calling into question the assumptions underlying our customary, habitual ways of thinking and acting and then being ready to think and act differently on the basis of this critical questioning." The process of taking a position is highly emotive and can leave us with a sense of joy and exhilaration, or with feelings of anxiety and uncertainty, as we explore new ways of looking at an issue. It also leads us to identify and challenge our assumptions, beliefs, values, and actions and thus to imagine and explore alternative ways of thinking about the controversy. By engaging in critical thinking, we confirm, refute, or modify our intuitions about what is the right or wrong position to take on an issue.

Stimulates Reflective Practice. Critical thinking fosters another important consequence of taking a position on a controversy: stimulation of reflective practice. Practice guided by critical reflection is grounded in the ability to scrutinize critically the actions, decisions, and justifications of our practice and diverse program offerings. Reflective practice allows us to become aware of the context in which we operate and to determine if the position we take is appropriate. Reflective practice is characterized by judgments that are appropriate for the set of circumstances in which we are operating (Cervero, 1988) and that provide us with an ethical foundation for our knowledge base regarding educational decisions, content selection, activities, evaluation criteria, social responsibility, and so forth. The action of taking a position is essential because it makes explicit the ethical dimensions that guide reflective practice.

Strengthening Our Own Position. The third consequence follows from the prior two consequences. By engaging in critical thinking and stimulating reflective analysis, adult educators are better able to understand and then argue within the framework of the range of alternatives of each issue or controversy. We become increasingly capable of wrestling with contrary ideas. However, the strength of the process of taking a position is the ability to sift through the concepts, words, and ideas of each alternative position and place them within a rational model that supports our chosen position. By understanding all sides of a controversy, we are better prepared to rebut arguments, whether philosophical or contextual, that oppose our position. While an understanding of opposing viewpoints helps us to gain an appreciation of alternative perspectives, it also enables us to gain a sound, logical, and reasonable foundation for the position that we actively pursue.

Distinguishing Between Controversies, Issues, and Problems

Up to this point, much of our discussion has focused on how controversies in adult and continuing education impact the field and associated practice. Controversies such as the purpose of adult and continuing education, professional certification, and the development of a code of ethics have dominated discussions in the field for some time, with dubious results. We suspect that future discussions will continue along the same path unless efforts are made by adult and continuing educators to move the debates to points of understanding and action. Part of the confusion and paralysis in dealing with various controversies may be a matter of semantics; that is, our terminology may unknowingly impede understanding as well as action.

The terms *controversy, issue,* and *problem* have much in common in that they all deal with the values, beliefs, and attitudes of adult educators. Yet, each term has a distinct meaning that, when clarified, can enable us to move from a point of ongoing discussion to points of deeper understanding and subsequent action.

As noted earlier, the term *controversy* refers to significant discussion marked by expression of opposing views. Certainly, there are abundant examples in the field of adult and continuing education where lines have been drawn on a particular controversy and elegant pleas made by supporters about the inherent superiority of their respective arguments. The debates during the 1980s over whether continuing professional education should be mandatory have a familiar ring. Yet, as long as the unit of analysis remains a controversy, only discussion will prevail. We believe that this is why most controversies in the field of adult and continuing education have remained stagnant, nice to discuss but difficult to solve.

If we move our unit of analysis from the controversy to the issue or issues associated with the controversy, a similar impasse will occur since an issue has similar characteristics to a controversy and may be defined as "a point or matter or discussion, debate or dispute" (*American Heritage Dictionary,* 1982, p. 680). Note how both terms emphasize discussion and debate. No wonder many practitioners in adult and continuing education remain on the sidelines, seeing little relevance to actionless debate.

However, if our unit of analysis shifts to the problem level where we can begin to understand the nature of the controversy, who controls the issue(s), and what needs to be done to solve the controversy, then we are in a better position to implement desired changes. By focusing on the problems associated with a given controversy, we move systematically from the realm of discussion to the realm of critical analysis and reflection and, finally, to a state of action. In short, controversies and their accompanying issues are debatable, whereas problems are solvable.

We believe that in order for the field of adult and continuing education to further develop, it must wrestle with the enduring controversies of its existence. In order to begin dealing with this conundrum, a model for understanding controversies in adult and continuing education is presented next with the aim of moving educators from a level of discussion to a level of action.

Controversy Valence Model

What is a model? According to the *American Heritage Dictionary* (1982, p. 806), a model is "a tentative description of a system or theory that accounts for all of its known properties." A model, in the context of adult and continuing education, can help to explicate the origins of a controversy and then introduce a logical step-by-step process whereby a deeper understanding of the problems associated with the controversy and subsequent action can take place. Remember that in order for a controversy to move to a point of resolution, we must first identify the impediments or problems that stand in the way of resolution. Sometimes these impediments are individual in nature, such as a person's philosophical stance regarding a state government's right to ensure competent performance by requiring a professional to continue to learn in order to maintain professional licensure. Other times the impediments are organizational in nature, such as the use of volunteers to teach in an adult basic education program who have no formal adult teacher training or certification from an accreditation agency because of limited budgets. The key, then, is to identify the problems or impediments in a controversy because, once identified, a range of action steps can be implemented to resolve the controversy. If the controversy is kept at a discussion level, as we have repeatedly pointed out, then no action can take place. While this situation may be tenable to some educators, it offends our collective judgment as professionals in the advancement of adult and continuing education practice.

The controversy valence model (Figure 1.1) begins with an identification of the controversy and a rationale as to why the controversy is of concern to the field. In building a rationale, the literature is consulted as well as expert opinion. Useful questions for consideration might include the following: How widespread is the controversy? Who is affected by it? Will the controversy handicap practitioners from doing their jobs? What is to be gained by eliminating the controversy?

Figure 1.1. Controversy Valence Model

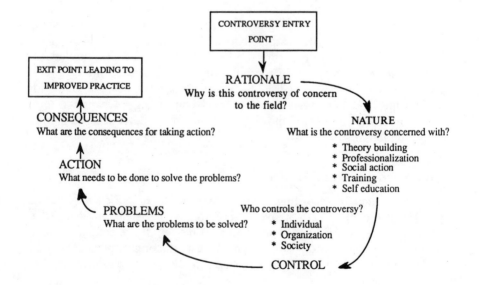

Once a rationale has been built to establish the basis of the controversy, the next step is to determine its nature. For example, does the controversy deal with professionalization, social action, training, or some combination of these? Let's say the controversy has to do with certification of adult educators. Currently, there is no universal certification procedure, although some states such as New York and California require training in adult education for teachers of adults. Some argue that professional certification is untenable because of the diversity of adult education providers and the fact that many programs are underfunded and rely on volunteers for delivery of services. Others argue that reliance on well-intentioned but untrained volunteers is one of the reasons that adult education continues to have only marginal status, which has hampered the field from gaining its rightful stature in the educational enterprise. Regardless of which side of the controversy one is on, the key here is an understanding of the nature of the controversy.

The next step in the model is to understand who controls the controversy. Is it controlled by the individual, organization, society, or some combination? For example, in the case of a code of ethics for adult and continuing educators, the factor of control figures at all three levels. Whereas for professional certification, control more likely impacts the organizational and societal levels, since both look to safeguard consumers and the general public against individual abuse.

Once the rationale, nature, and control of a controversy are understood, the model then enables us to identify the problems that need to be solved. In the case of professional certification, many problems can be identified: Should all adult educators be certified or only specific subgroups? Who will do the certifying—an umbrella organization such as the American Association for Adult and Continuing Education, a special interest organization such as the American Society for Training and Development, or an independent agency? How will enforcement be implemented? Will only certified adult educators be permitted to work in publicly supported programs? How long will certification last and what means will be used to maintain certification?

After the range of problems to be solved are identified, the next step in the model is to move to the action phase: What needs to be done to solve the problems? Here, emphasis is placed on strategic identification of the action steps that result in desired changes. Sometimes the changes can be accomplished quickly, whereas other times they may take much longer. The important point is to analyze and then implement both short- and long-range goals so that desired outcomes are accomplished.

The final step in the model is to analyze the consequences of taking action. Here, the emphasis is on not only the desired or positive consequences but also the negative and unintended consequences. Many times, we focus our efforts on positive outcomes, thinking that these are the only by-products of desired action. However, there may be negative or unintended, damaging consequences as well. These should be considered in the overall implementation phase, thereby strengthening our efforts in the long run.

Conclusion

The field of adult and continuing education is at an important juncture in its development. There are numerous controversies in the field begging for reasoned judgment and action. In the volume chapters that follow, many of these controversies are debated by noted experts positing arguments both for and against particular positions. It is our hope that the controversy valence model presented above will not only clarify the vexing controversies of our day but also lead to constructive action. The hallmark of any developing discipline is its ability to critically analyze where it has come from and where it is going in the future. Part of that analysis is before us today. Please join us on the journey of confronting our controversies in challenging times.

References

American Heritage Dictionary. (2nd ed.) Boston: Houghton Mifflin, 1982.

Beder, H. *Adult Literacy: Issues for Policy and Practice.* Malabar, Fla.: Krieger, 1991.

Boggs, D. L. "Philosophies at Issue." In B. W. Kreitlow and Associates, *Examining Controversies in Adult Education.* San Francisco: Jossey-Bass, 1981.

Brockett, R. G. (ed.). *Ethical Issues in Adult Education.* New York: Teachers College Press, 1988.

Brockett, R. G., and Hiemstra, R. *Self-Direction in Adult Learning.* New York: Routledge & Kegan Paul, 1991.

Brookfield, S. D. *Developing Critical Thinkers: Challenging Adults to Explore Alternative Ways of Thinking and Acting.* San Francisco: Jossey-Bass, 1987.

Candy, P. C. *Self-Direction for Lifelong Learning: A Comprehensive Guide to Theory and Practice.* San Francisco: Jossey-Bass, 1991.

Cervero, R. M. *Effective Continuing Education for Professionals.* San Francisco: Jossey-Bass, 1988.

Collins, M. *Adult Education as Vocation.* New York: Routledge & Kegan Paul, 1991.

Frankena, W. D. "A Model for Analyzing a Philosophy of Education." In J. Park (ed.), *Selected Readings in the Philosophy of Education.* New York: Macmillan, 1974.

Galbraith, M. W. (ed.). *Adult Learning Methods.* Malabar, Fla.: Krieger, 1990.

Galbraith, M. W. (ed.). *Facilitating Adult Learning.* Malabar, Fla.: Krieger, 1991.

Hiemstra, R., and Sisco, B. R. *Individualizing Instruction: Making Learning Personal, Empowering, and Successful.* San Francisco: Jossey-Bass, 1990.

Kreitlow, B. W. "Preface." In B. W. Kreitlow and Associates, *Examining Controversies in Adult Education.* San Francisco: Jossey-Bass, 1981.

Merriam, S. B., and Caffarella, R. S. *Learning in Adulthood: A Comprehensive Guide.* San Francisco: Jossey-Bass, 1991.

Mezirow, J. *Transformative Dimensions of Adult Learning.* San Francisco: Jossey-Bass, 1991.

Quigley, B. A. (ed.). *Fulfilling the Promise of Adult and Continuing Education.* New Directions for Adult and Continuing Education, no. 44. San Francisco: Jossey-Bass, 1989.

Ross-Gordon, J., Martin, L., and Briscoe, D. B. (eds.). *Serving Culturally Diverse Populations.* New Directions for Adult and Continuing Education, no. 48. San Francisco: Jossey-Bass, 1990.

Schön, D. A. *Educating the Reflective Practitioner: Toward a New Design for Teaching and Learning in the Professions.* San Francisco: Jossey-Bass, 1987.

Vroom, V. H. *Work and Motivation.* New York: Wiley, 1964.

Webster's Ninth New Collegiate Dictionary. Springfield, Mass.: Merriam-Webster, 1991.

MICHAEL W. GALBRAITH *is associate professor of adult education and coordinator of graduate studies in adult education at Temple University, Philadelphia.*

BURTON R. SISCO *is associate professor of adult education and coordinator of the graduate program in adult and postsecondary education at the University of Wyoming, Laramie.*

PART ONE

Should the Starting Point of
Adult and Continuing Education
Be to Change the Individual
or Society?

A framework is presented to assist readers in reviewing their own positions on the appropriate starting point, focal point, and ending point for adult and continuing education.

The Undeniable Link:
Adult and Continuing Education
and Individual Change

Paulette T. Beatty

It is informative to reflect on one's own position on an adult education issue and the underlying values and personal experiences that have given rise to the position. It is challenging to hold this position up to critical scrutiny, to explore its soundness in light of questions posed by the profession and society, and to analyze its potential for the improvement of practice.

In this chapter, I argue from both a professional and a societal perspective that the individual and change within the individual are not only the necessary and sufficient beginning and ending points for all adult education but also the focal points for the educational undertaking. It is at this level of change alone that all adult educators can rightly be held accountable both by the profession and the society that it serves. First, however, I present a brief look at the evolution of my own personal position on this issue.

Evolution of a Personal Position

My personal position has evolved over almost four decades of working in adult education. I have taken during this period two decidedly different paths. Yet, in retrospect, these distinct paths have proved to be complementary forces in the shaping of my position as a professional.

Early in my own journey into adulthood thirty-six years ago, my first career choice involved the nonformal adult religious education arena. My early values as an adult educator and change agent were formed through

New Directions for Adult and Continuing Education, no. 54, Summer 1992 © Jossey-Bass Publishers

two major roles that I played over approximately eighteen years. In the first role, I guided young adults in the early stages of their own vocational, career, and academic paths as women in a religious community. In the second role of managing a regional retreat and renewal center for adults, I also was engaged in the design and evaluation of a myriad of educational programs and in the direct facilitation of learning. During this period, I came to appreciate the critical importance of understanding where individuals are as they embark on and progress through their journeys of personal change. I learned that relationships of trust had to be established and sustained if I was to be welcomed as a mentor into the personal worlds of these individuals, and that unless these mutually respectful relationships were developed within environments designed for change, change and the process of growth either did not begin, faltered in the absence of support during the early, arduous stages of the process, or else was not fully consolidated into personal repertoires. A commitment to personal change for individuals became my insignia.

My next transition was into another eighteen-year phase of my professional career, which brings me to the present. This phase has wholly engaged me in formal, rather than nonformal, adult education, functioning exclusively within higher education. First, having decided to pursue answers to questions that had surrounded my professional practice, I turned to the academic community and became a student of adult education, adding a new dimension to my academic background and a new foundation for my experiential understanding of the phenomenon of adult learning and change. Then, subsequent to my studies, I assumed the role of an academician, helping to shape experiences and environments for other individuals in order to assist them in their individual processes of becoming leaders within the profession of adult education. Through these years, I was again reminded of the formative power of individual mentoring relationships. However, to this conviction I added another, that the key to unlocking the door to change resides within individuals. The process of professional development ultimately depends on an individual's aspirations, hard work, willingness to change, and belief that he or she can make a difference. A commitment to professional change for individuals became my insignia.

Arguments from the Professional Perspective

A number of questions are raised in regard to the personal position that I have articulated above. How do we define our profession? What are the foci of the various theories of adult learning and development? What undergirds the array of philosophical stances espoused by members of our profession? And what are the fundamental principles of ethical decision making that shape our field of practice?

Definition of the Field. The field of adult education involves a never-ending process of reformulating its definition, as a review of field handbooks reveals. Schroeder (1970) starts this process by reviewing approaches for defining the field, including classification, structural analysis, and operation analysis. He refrains from offering his own definition; however, in reviewing the classification and operation analysis approaches, one deduces that purposive change within the individual is the sole, central, and universally present construct. Structural analysis does little to advance the discussion other than to situate practitioners in their arena within the field as a whole.

Boyd and Apps (1980) continue with efforts to redefine the discipline by presenting a three-dimensional model in which transactional modes define the manner in which adults are grouped for learning. Client focus specifies the primary beneficiary of the educational undertaking; and personal, social, and cultural systems highlight the contexts within which the lives of adult learners are embedded. Although their model assists the profession in exploring the diverse configurations and manifestations that the field of adult education might take, it fails to make explicit the common thread. Implicit in the model is the notion that the basic unit of change, without which neither education nor learning occurs, must always be the individual.

For seasoned practitioners and those entering the profession, Courtney (1989, p. 24) offered the following definition: "Adult education is an intervention into the ordinary business of life—an intervention whose immediate goal is change, in knowledge or in competence." For the field as a whole, we can define our niche as professionals by saying that we help others change in knowledge, skills, and affect, and that these capacities then empower them within their worlds. Surely, adult education has emphasized its commitment to the individual and the individual change process.

Learning and Development Theories. In reviewing the array of extant theories relevant to adult learning and development, I am impressed with not only the diversity of perspectives represented but also the common theme running throughout (Boucouvalas and Krupp, 1989; Merriam, 1987). The unit of analysis for these theories is the individual, regardless of the type of change that is expounded, and all present explanatory systems for change on the individual level. The essential theoretical underpinnings of our profession and our field of practice of adult education relate to characteristics that are inherent to the individual. This is not to say, of course, that there are no other relevant theoretical bases from which our professional practice can and, at times, should draw, but rather that we would be irresponsible if we denied the centrality of the individual at all points in the change process. The Commission of Professors of Adult Education recently developed a set of standards indicating, among other things, the essential elements of curricula in graduate programs. These standards grew out of a concern to ensure the development and preservation of the knowledge base for the profession. They emphasize, as minimums, the provision of a robust understanding of adult learning and development, and of the essential competencies associated with effective facilitation of learning, development and evaluation of learning experiences, and management of educational enterprises. Surely, other elements can and should be added as institutional mandates dictate and institutional resources allow. Yet, graduate programs increasingly will be held accountable for developing individual leaders for the profession who possess the knowledge, attitudes, and competencies essential for responsible practice. Further, these core elements must be focused on the nature of learning, the individual learner, and the management and facilitation of individual change.

Philosophical Stances. The philosophical stances adopted by reflective practitioners in the field of adult education are not homogeneous. Some believe that education should be directed toward the emancipation of the minds and spirits of individuals, thus enabling them fully to benefit from the collective beauty and wisdom contained within our societal heritage. Others believe that education should be directed toward the development of individuals with predetermined standards of capabilities and behaviors in order to produce a quality-controlled output of goods or services. Yet others hold that education should be directed toward the full development of the innate potential of individuals in all of their dimensions in order to produce fully actualized persons. And still others hold that education must be fundamentally utilitarian and directed toward the development of functional individuals with relevant skills that can be directly applied in their everyday social roles, ultimately resulting in the improvement of the structures of the social system in which they live. All of these stances predicate a goal in which the individual is changed in one way or another by virtue of participation in educational experiences, whereby the second-order effects of this change necessarily impact the world in which these individuals live. Again, the individual is central to the fundamental values of education, and all philosophical stances are directed toward the empowerment of the individual in one capacity or another.

Ethical Principles. The most fundamental principles of ethical decision making are applicable to this discussion. As professionals and practitioners within the society, we are bound by unwritten principles that have shaped the emergence of our profession. Even though we lack a uniform code of ethics to guide practice, we are ethically compelled both to secure benefits for our clients and to protect them from harm. First, our constituencies have a right to expect of us a functional competence in the application of the knowledge base germane to the field. Second, they have a right to expect positive change for themselves individually, in knowledge, skills, and attitudes. Finally, they have a right to expect that they personally will benefit from and will not be harmed by participation in our educational programs. In sum, these expectations derive from contractual obligations that we, as adult educators, have assumed with respect to the individual learners whom we have attracted to our programs.

Arguments from the Societal Perspective

Focusing on the major social sectors—economic, political, and social— within our society, we encounter a number of different arguments from each perspective.

Economic Perspective. Education is a valuable commodity in our society. Further, this commodity is both mobile and inseparable from individual persons who are its sole possessors. In addition, the possession of this commodity readily translates into numerous benefits to individuals in terms of income, status, housing, life-style, and health and well-being. Corporations spend untold amounts from their training and development budgets in order to ensure a competitive edge. It is imperative that all employees perform effectively on the job. Employee assistance officers, human resources development directors, workplace literacy personnel, and human relations and communications training ombudsmen abound in corporate America. Certainly, it is difficult to discern just who is the prime beneficiary of these specific training initiatives. Is it the sponsor or the individual employee? Insofar as the employee is retained within the corporation, perhaps we could speak of the employer as the prime beneficiary, or perhaps we should speak of the employer and the employee as equal beneficiaries. However, when the employee leaves that setting, the employer ceases to be a beneficiary in any regard, and the employee has become enhanced with intrinsic capacities of knowledge, attitudes, and skills that increase his or her attractiveness to another potential employer. Of course, the corporation, having engaged responsibly in this training, might be buying itself freedom from future failure-to-train litigation, or it could be positioning itself to function with greater effectiveness and efficiency in getting its people on line and could become a well-recognized employee-friendly corporation, investing in its personnel as a win-win undertaking. A full detailing of who the beneficiaries are in this scenario would require a comprehensive cost-benefit analysis. However, what is not in question is that the focus throughout is on individuals in need of interventions, on individuals in the process of development, and on explicit change at the level of the individual.

Political Perspective. The espoused function of government is to ensure the social order and the preservation of the rights of the members of the society for the good of all. For example, the media are replete with reports on public efforts within our society to ensure all citizens the right to work. Age, gender, religion, ethnicity, or disability cannot be considered as factors in the decision to employ, promote, or dismiss an individual. Rather, the determining factor, by law, is whether or not the individual has within himself or herself the basic knowledge, attitudes or dispositions, and competencies needed to perform the job. In fact, virtually all of the publicly sponsored adult education taking place today in our society is directed at providing those basic capabilities to individuals. The federal government has been working for over twenty-five years through entitlements of the Adult Education Act to ensure literacy among adults; for, indeed, if individuals are to function effectively in our increasingly complex society, they must be functionally literate. When a local, publicly funded community counseling center provides help to families through parenting skills workshops, or when the Cooperative Extension Service develops a wide range of educational programs and support services for distressed farm families, or when amnesty programs are put in place for newly arrived members of our society, individuals are being taken at teachable moments, moments ripe for transformation, and are being empowered one by one. Each individual is being provided with some of the basic means needed to meet the challenges of his or her life. Is society the beneficiary when its citizens are developed and provided the rights to earn a living, to sustain themselves in difficult family and economic times, and to learn to function in a totally new world? Yes, undoubtedly, but it is the individuals who are capacitated and who will ultimately form an educated citizenry for an improved society.

Social Perspective. How does the public at large view our role, and in what ways do they hold us accountable? As many of the promotional brochures for continuing professional education workshops and conferences cross my desk, I am struck by what, from a marketing perspective, is promised to the participants. Participants will be fortified with an array of skills to apply in professional settings. Yet, not long ago, investigative reporting revealed the mockery that is made at times of the continuing professional education conference. Some professional group treks off to an exotic resort for ten, twenty, or thirty continuing education units, rarely, if ever, engages in an educational activity, and then writes the trip off as a deductible educational expense associated with a business enterprise. Is it not the expectation of the certification agencies or associations and the general public at large that practice will be improved, that the client or consumer will be protected by these purported efforts to ensure the competence of licensed practitioners? In this instance, most persons would agree that improved skills for practice settings should be accruing directly to the professionals and should, ultimately, translate to more effective service to the consumer.

When adults seek us out for education, whether in the area of technical preparation, stress management, leadership development, advocacy skills, health enhancement, or leisure pursuits, they are coming to us because we are professionals who effect change for individuals. When we are approached by corporations to design and conduct retirement planning workshops, to evaluate the efficacy of in-house training programs, and to implement systems supporting wellness for employees, we are sought out because of our competence in effecting change—new knowledge, new behaviors, new attitudes—for individuals. Employees will directly benefit and corporations will be improved. When we join with others in the community to address concerns confronting the common well-being, or are invited to shape community forums for local school issues, we bring with us a unique perspective to add to the solution, skills in understanding how change might best be effected, and skills in designing effective interventions as part of a comprehensive approach to solve problems or address common concerns. Others may well be more knowledgeable about the substantive issues under consideration; we, as adult educators, however, shape experiences and environments for individuals to foster change.

Path to Excellence

Throughout, we have been exploring a single question: What is the universally appropriate mission for adult education within our society today? This mission need not diminish the flourishing philosophical, social, and political diversity within the field, which we prize for its responsiveness within a democratic society. Rather, the identification of this mission will help us to understand more clearly the essential elements at the core of our profession, to interpret and present ourselves more accurately to our public, and to advance the profession beyond its current level of development as a social entity. It will help us to articulate that about which we must stand in union; and it will provide us wide berth to flourish in our unique practice arenas.

The issue remains about the starting, focal, and ending points of adult education: the individual and change within the individual or the society and change within the society. It is my view that this dichotomy is false. Can we have the individual and change within the individual as the prime perspective within our arenas of practice as adult educators and still execute our responsibilities as adult educators? I argue that we can and must. But so long as individuals are empowered, the process of change cannot be contained; it continues on into ever-increasing spheres of individual activity to exercise influence beyond our wildest imaginations. There will be change on multiple levels because of our involvement with the change of real individuals in real-world contexts. For me personally, however, I count success one individual at a time.

References

Boucouvalas, M., and Krupp, J.-A. "Adult Development and Learning." In S. B. Merriam and P. M. Cunningham (eds.), *Handbook of Adult and Continuing Education*. San Francisco: Jossey-Bass, 1989.

Boyd, R. D., and Apps, J. W. "A Conceptual Model for Adult Education." In R. D. Boyd and J. W. Apps (eds.), *Redefining the Discipline of Adult Education*. San Francisco: Jossey-Bass, 1980.

Courtney, S. "Defining Adult and Continuing Education." In S. B. Merriam and P. M. Cunningham (eds.), *Handbook of Adult and Continuing Education*. San Francisco: Jossey-Bass, 1989.

Merriam, S. B. "Adult Learning and Theory Building: A Review." *Adult Education Quarterly*, 1987, 37 (4), 187–198.

Schroeder, W. L. "Adult Education Defined and Described." In R. M. Smith, G. F. Aker, and J. R. Kidd (eds.), *Handbook of Adult Education*. New York: Macmillan, 1970.

PAULETTE T. BEATTY *is associate professor and coordinator of adult and extension education, Texas A&M University, College Station.*

Adult and continuing education should accept the role of agent for change, creator of the future, and designer of social missions.

The Undeniable Link:
Adult and Continuing Education
and Social Change

Paul J. Ilsley

This chapter is based on the loaded question, Should the starting point of adult and continuing education be to change the individual or society? The question brings to bear an impressive array of issues regarding the visions, missions, and politics of adult and continuing education, as well as how and why we plan programs the way that we do. However, it is important to recognize the shortcomings of the question. An obvious shortcoming is that there are more than two "starting points." Examples abound in the organizational arena: to strengthen a corporate organization, to plan an agenda for a professional association, to sell a product. Another problem is that the two starting points identified could be pursued at the same time. The question poses a false dualism.

Dualisms often encourage people to consider two extreme positions of an argument, as though there are only two opposing sides. Too often the extremes force people toward middle ground, as if one extreme is too conservative and the other too liberal. I believe that this result would be most unfortunate in this case, as it would be in any false dualism, because such a reaction would limit other arguments and ideas, many of which could be more compelling or creative. There are numerous dimensions to the question posed here. With recognition of the shifting contextual issues associated with individualism and collectivism, and what those terms mean to adult educators, it is challenging to assume that they reside on opposite ends of a continuum. In the context of adult education, both are indispensable. There is no such thing as pure individualistic education. After all, adult learning

New Directions for Adult and Continuing Education, no. 54, Summer 1992 © Jossey-Bass Publishers

occurs within a larger frame of action, such as a group, institution, society, or culture. Education that encourages individual growth does so within a social context and is conducted in a way that is restricted by, connected with, framed around, or nestled in a larger social arena. Likewise, there is no such thing as purely social or collective education. Without individual learning and action, there would be no vision, no mission, and no future. Without a mission to guide it, education is meaningless. Without individual learning, education is impossible. Although the argument is abstract and academic, my aim in this chapter is to stimulate discussion beyond the extremes. Quite often, opposing views are not extremes at all but rather the beginning points for more creative questioning.

Since the inception of the field, adult educators have planned programs based on at least two kinds of missions: those that preserve the status quo and those that call for change or improvement of the social condition. My purpose here is to make a case for why adult educators should openly accept the role as agent for change, creator of the future, designer of social missions. Especially during these times of accelerated political and social change, when the future is increasingly uncertain, the need to examine the purposes and visions of the field is acute. How we as adult educators attend to current and future societal problems is central to our sense of professionalism. Accordingly, the three objectives of this chapter are (1) to articulate a position on the importance of societal visions to the field of adult education; (2) to demonstrate that mainstream adult education has changed over time, and that both an improved society and improved practice are the likely outcomes; and (3) to point out several distinctive and unusual implications for practice.

Reflections on the Social Mission of Adult Education

I was raised to believe that so long as I am honest and work hard, I will be successful. As a young white male from an upper-middle-class family, I was largely unaware that this Calvinist ethic would serve me better than it would others. I believed the assumption that education can be both equal and excellent and that inequality can be alleviated with increased attention to excellent education. I thought that success was a function of individual merit and action. Now, I believe that these conclusions are premature. Not everyone has a fair chance at success. The advantages of privilege are great. Of course, it is *possible* for a person to start with nothing and become wealthy in this country, and there is freedom for individual initiative. Undeniably, there are positive and negative aspects of freedom in a modern technological culture.

Our educational system operates in much the same way as the work world. The merit system and credentialization processes in the United States favor people who are proficient with the language of the dominant culture, who are agile with bureaucracies, and who are comfortable with standardized tests such as the Scholastic Aptitude Test and Graduate Record Examination. For those who were not born into the middle class, a game of catch-up must be played; and while we in the dominant culture exert individual initiative, those who are learning the rules remain behind. The educational system says that in order for a person to succeed, someone else must fail. For the grade A to mean anything, there must also be the grades D and F. Whoever gets the best grades wins the best opportunities and the highest credentials, such as an Ivy League B.A., Ph.D., or M.D. In practice, education is not both equal and excellent for every student.

Education is a curious phenomenon because it has both controlling and liberating sides. The controlling side includes the presentation to individuals of more than eight years of subject matter, or overt curriculum. More controlling than subject matter, however, is the covert curriculum, or umpteen years of training in punctuality, obedience, rote memorization, and competition. In this way, schools "manufacture" soldiers of production for the work force, especially industry, and for other places in which these attributes are appreciated. The liberating side of education transcends bureaucracy and systematic inequality and helps people to understand themselves, their rituals, and their values. For me, the most perplexing aspect of being an educator is coming to grips with the fact that formal education can, at one and the same time, control and liberate people.

Ethical Considerations of Common, Nonelitist Adult Education

Missions change over time, gaining new properties and growing gradually, almost imperceptibly. There is a growing uneasiness and impatience among educators with many taken-for-granted assumptions about the world, our field of practice, what it means to be a professor, and the reward structures that guide us. Over time, we forget that in the world outside of the ivory tower there are tumbles and falls that people in universities may never experience. Still, I am very optimistic about the future. Many of the characteristics of adult education that draw me closer to it, such as its spontaneity, flexibility, and energy, are ever present. What frustrates me is that a coherent social ideology is missing from our mission statement. I deeply believe that our policies and practices would be enriched by the inclusion of a central and profound sense of social justice in our mission.

I cannot be sure when these ethical considerations first occurred to me. Perhaps it was in relation to my study of futurism and voluntary action and their respective intersections with adult education. Through study and practice in these areas of interest, I cultivated the following set of ethical considerations that guides my teaching and program planning in adult education:

Anticipatory Planning. This type of planning is essential today because of the accelerating nature of change. In this sense, adult educators can learn from futurists.

Participatory Planning. This type of planning is required for social missions of any meaning to be accomplished. Adult learning is a key ingredient in participatory politics, and vice versa.

Social and Political Enfranchisement. This is a right of everyone and must be tolerated in order for a democracy to survive. Adult educators deepen the democratic spirit by fostering this ethic.

Accountability to the Public. Although we are held accountable to our funding agents for the money that we receive, there are times when the accountability criteria (types of reporting) that we use to assess our programs may not coincide with the best part of our social mission. There are many aspects of our work that cannot be measured. The most important accountability criteria are those that are most appreciated by the public, not by bureaucrats.

Advocacy. Adult educators can learn from members of voluntary agencies who realize that in any element of service there is a spirit of advocacy. The very heart of the mission of adult education may be to bring voice to disenfranchised groups of people.

These ethical considerations serve adult educators because they guide efforts to equalize the disparities among people that exist within any modern technological culture. If adult education is to grow into a profession that is fair to all people, it will take more than these few ideas to accomplish the task. It will take awareness of cultural differences and cultural tolerance.

My visit to China was a critical event for me because it clarified, for the first time, many things that I had previously taken for granted. Differences in language, music, food, and dress are obvious. What are more difficult to comprehend are the subtle aspects of culture, such as notions of modesty, conceptions of beauty, ideals governing child rearing, patterns of superior-subordinate relations, gift giving, definitions of justice, incentives to work, notions of leadership, patterns of group decision making, conceptions of cleanliness, attitudes toward dependent people, approaches to problem solving, conceptions of status mobility, eye contact, social roles in relation to status by age, sex, class, and occupation, conceptions of past and future, definitions of education, nature of friendship, ordering of time, conceptions of self, preference for competition or cooperation, body language, and notions about logic and validity. The nature of our respective languages has everything to do with how we conceptualize and order our lives; thus, to understand another person, we must first speak a similar language.

Adult education is an indispensable condition of modern economic and scientific development in China. Adult education is viewed as a means of elevating the country into the modern technological world; it is expected to serve directly as a means of improving the quality of the labor force, and it is an important channel through which to advance culture and ideology. As is true of adult education in the United States, there is no standardization of terminology in China. Basically, adult education there is defined as organized programs of learning for adults that contribute to the long-term aims of the government.

The lessons can be brought home. Even though I do not speak Chinese, I understand now that subtle definitional differences must also be grasped in order for effective communication to occur. Moreover, one does not have to leave home to visit a Third World country. Many places in the United States offer distinct types of Third World cultural differences. If we adult educators hope to communicate effectively with the people whom we are supposed to serve, we must understand that there are linguistic differences among groups in the United States, and that not all people are members of the middle or upper class.

The importance of understanding multiculturalism is not so much that we can better serve Third World people, whether abroad or at home. Rather, it is to learn compassion for all of humanity, and hatred of inequality, prejudice, or injustice of any kind, in order to reach the people who are most in need of contact—the rich and powerful. We are striving to educate the wrong class of people. The people who need to learn the most about social injustice are politicians, industrialists, and prominent leaders of bureaucracies. What they need to know is what people of color, the homeless, and immigrants, among others, in the United States already understand.

Centrality of Social Visions in the Field of Adult Education

Where are the boundaries of adult education? What do we admit into the field as "mainstream" and what do we exclude? Through examination of the various purposes of adult education, we can better position ourselves to reflect on what we do and to see the relevance of our actions in ways that we have never seen before. In theory, the logical starting point for the planning of programs in adult education is the vision, or the mission, whether in literacy, continuing education, political action, human resources development, or any other area of practice. Visions are either normative (that is, doing what we do now, only better) or they are idealistic, leading us toward life-styles that are holistically different and, hopefully, an improvement over those that we have now. Either way, visions refer to a societal state of affairs, because even the most individualistic visions reside within a social, political, economic, and cultural context.

Of course, not all programs begin with the establishment of a vision with substantive meaning; and even if they did, visions are sometimes forgotten or abandoned, or they simply evolve to a different place. The mission by default in adult education is to meet the individual needs of learners and to follow the "bean counters" in state and federal bureaucracies (Collins, 1991). It is not so much that individualism is a problem. After all, missions require individual thinking, reflecting, and acting. Individualism and collectivism are inexorably linked. But by itself, individualism is not enough to change the inequities and societal misalignments that threaten our future. As Collins (1991) infers, at its incipient stage, the field of adult education was guided by visions of professionalism, of shaking off its marginal status and becoming a legitimate field of practice and study. Our initial visions of the future were, perhaps, excessively prudent, because our own survival was at stake. We included into our ranks people who basically accepted the vision that society is healthy, and even if it is not, it is not the business of adult education to do anything about it. We still act in this excessively prudent way; old habits die hard. But our ranks include activists of many kinds and individuals with a deep sense of commitment toward social improvement. Evidence to support this contention can be seen in the types of papers that are presented at conferences and in our literature. More than ever, adult educators are expressing a sense of commitment toward social purpose (Hart, Meyer, Laughlin, and Karlovic, 1991; Peterson, 1991).

Should adult educators foster societal visions in a way that is different from what we are doing now? Of course. Adult educators recognize the transformative nature of the life experience (Lindeman, [1926] 1961; Brookfield, 1986). But transformation is not easily measured, and therefore it is not easily funded. It is not as if individual choice does not matter. It does. Since our individual choices reside within a larger societal context, the way that we make changes for individuals generally follows that implicit vision of society.

Adult educators are agents for making the world a better place. The visions of the field of adult education are not difficult to understand. Many come to mind that sound familiar, such as the vision of lifelong learning by all members of our society. In this vision, learning is seen as a ubiquitous and powerful force to improve citizenship, families, and professions. Another is the vision of service, whereby those in need receive care and attention during the crises that they face. In every curriculum that we plan and every text we use, there is an implicit, if not explicit, assumption about the future and why a learner will be better off knowing, feeling, or doing things differently.

Less obvious visions in adult education include equality of workers, civil rights, peace and justice, ecological fairness. Many adult educators believe in such visions, though as a field we have shied away from declaring overt political intentions. Officially, we embrace critical thinking, but we refrain from identifying and acting on specific political plans of action. Historical accounts of adult education, until recently, ignored groups of people who were countercultural or resisted the status quo. Arguably, the largest adult education movement of the nineteenth century was the Freed-man's Bureau. Enormous amounts of funding and effort were required to provide transitional programs to millions of former slaves so that they might adjust to life in post–Civil War America (Morris, 1981; Rachal, 1986). There has not been another national program of such scale or purpose since. Yet, where does it appear in our literature? Where are the historical accounts of black adult educators, Hispanic adult educators, laborers, ethnic leaders, or equal rights activists? By excluding the stories of marginalized people, we miss a great opportunity to expand our sense of vision. We learn that the stories of the dominant culture, particularly those of white males, are the basis of the mission of adult education. Fortunately, a number of historians are interested in filling in the gaps of unacknowledged adult education (Altenbaugh, 1990; Hellyer, 1988; Schied, 1991; Welton, 1987; Zacharakis-Jutz, 1991). Their research will eventually alter our perceptions of what adult education and adult learning have meant to people who have only recently been acknowledged by historians of adult education.

I am interested in studying the phenomenon of social commitment. In this topic, I see an interesting junction between the field of adult education and social movements. Commitment occupies a central place in adult edu-cation, though it is not a frequent topic of discussion or research. Commit-ment is a crucial aspect, individually and organizationally, of the human experience. Commitment varies in intensity and is multidirectional; people often feel competing loyalties, such as client well-being versus maintenance of the organizational structure, belief in the mission versus the comfort and goodness of the organizational group. These kinds of conflicts of commit-ment influence motivation and action, including a person's duration of loyalty (Ilsley, 1990).

Simply to ask why a person participates in adult education, in learning situations, or in social action is not sufficient to uncover the deep aspects of commitment because discourse on one's own values is rarely offered at such a superficial level. On the one hand, when we express our motivation, we do so with our actions. We usually are able to reflect on those actions and understand our motivation. On the other hand, even though actions may be an expression of commitment, in order to understand our actions, we must juxtapose them with our value structures. In motivation, there is a reward structure. In commitment, we act on our beliefs. Granted, the differ-ences between the two are slippery, but comprehension of them brings clarity to the *meaning* of social participation, citizenship, and civic learning.

I had the opportunity to interview and observe volunteers in urban, suburban, and rural areas in such organizations as neighborhood groups, groups that provide free housing for people with AIDS, peace groups, and feminist groups. I learned that there are many focal points of commitment, though they tend to cluster in four groupings: commitment to self, to orga-nization, to others (students and clients), and to social mission. The nature of commitment to these clusters differ markedly among them, evoking varying degrees of sacrifice, prompting various kinds of conflict, and providing different challenges. There are a number of trade-offs, including what are perhaps the most pressing, the client-organization trade-off and the group-social vision trade-off. These extenuating trade-offs are by-products of the limited effectiveness of attempts to organize free will. An understanding of commitment furnishes adult educators with an appreciation of the values that drive social participation, the creation of a sense of mission, and, indeed, learning.

Effective Practice Is Guided by Forceful Social Visions

There is an old saying that though we may never reach the stars, we can guide our ships by them. In the same sense, many social visions of adult educators, such as peace, justice, and equality, are seemingly unreachable ideals. But these limits should not deter our efforts. Adult education is a future-oriented field of practice that is designed essentially to help people face the future. What future is most desirable to adult educators? The question is compelling because what is desirable to one person may be controlling and delimiting to another. Certain images of the future favor only certain groups of people, depending on the values contained in and served by those images. Our future will probably be determined by the powerful, such as leaders in the Pentagon, on Wall Street and Madison Avenue, and in the White House. But there is no force greater than the will of the people in determining the future. We can be the architects, the planners, and the implementors of the future. Adult educators, like any citizens, can abdicate their right to be determinants of the future, especially if they trust the values of those in positions of power. But it is a basic right of citizens in this country to become involved when they see a better way.

The main implication for practice is that, no matter what, educators are guided by a vision. Even if we take it for granted, we serve a mission or some sort of vision of the future, in every country, in every school, and in every classroom. Moreover, visions of adult education are inextricably linked with the visions of society that we share and work toward realizing (Tough, 1991). Additional implications for adult education may result if we take a strong common stance for social betterment. For example, we could open a dialogue with people who have been excluded from traditional programs, provide policymakers with realistic accountability criteria, and find ways of addressing common societal and global issues. If we so decide, we can put our minds to work on a number of issues, such as environmental concerns and social inequality. But it is clear that adult education will not be part of the solution if we do not start with a vision or image of what we want to achieve.

Adult education has tremendous drive, but no direction. We have a wonderful capacity to get to where we are going, if we only knew where. The time has come for us to realize that we are not a marginal field of practice anymore, and that we do not have to be guided by the status quo. American adult education has been overly concerned with reliability, methodology, and socially responsible behavior. Today, social change commands attention. Social relevance is the demand from both within and outside the field. It is to our advantage that adult education is a constantly moving, tension-filled, and fluctuating field of practice, for this dynamism and flexibility enable us to discover and respond to a myriad of social problems. But as long as we employ a content-centered approach to teaching adults, as if facts are neutral and values lie beyond our domain, the prominence of the values of the dominant culture is inevitable and implicit agreement with the visions of the status quo is maintained. In this way, we perpetuate the same problems that we attempt to address. To what extent has adult education brought us closer to solving some of society's enormous difficulties?

Awareness of central values is a crucial first step toward the achievement of a social agenda and the conscious creation of the future. Values are future oriented because, by definition, they guide us toward a value-laden future. Someone once told me that probably nothing we ever do will make any real difference, but it is actually essential that we act anyway. Similarly, we probably shall never realize our dreams. But that should not prevent us from trying.

Appreciation of cultural differences and the north-south issues outside of and within the country are two critical concerns for adult educators with social vision. To extend awareness, and to help others to tolerate pluralism, it is imperative to first recognize the beauty of diversity among people at home. The striving for social justice and equality is tantamount to the creation of space for people who normally do not enroll in traditional programs, such as minority persons and people with minority perspectives, leaders of labor unions, feminists, and peace activists. One does not need to visit a foreign country to learn what cultural diversity means, although it helps.

Appreciation for equality is a fundamental aspect of the mission of adult education. Adult education is in a better position than most other social institutions, including the government, to serve the interests of the people, because it strives for self-sufficiency of the citizenry. Many actually believe that in the United States there is liberty and justice for all. But neither liberty nor justice are functions of individualism. No amount of individualism and bureaucratic accountability can lead to social justice. In order to help secure a just world, adult educators must do more than increase their competence in programming and their displays of compassion; they must go beyond business as usual. It certainly will take a lot more than increased attention to individualism.

References

Altenbaugh, R. J. *Education for Struggle: The American Labor Colleges of the 1920s and 1930s.* Philadelphia: Temple University Press, 1990.

Brookfield, S. D. *Understanding and Facilitating Adult Learning: A Comprehensive Analysis of Principles and Effective Practices.* San Francisco: Jossey-Bass, 1986.

Collins, M. *Adult Education as Vocation.* New York: Routledge & Kegan Paul, 1991.

Hart, M., Meyer, S., Laughlin, K., and Karlovic, N. "Reconstructing the Adult Education Enterprise: The Value of Feminist Theory to Adult Education." In *The Proceedings of the Adult Education Research Conference.* Norman: University of Oklahoma, 1991.

Hellyer, M. R. "A Marxist Analysis of the Contributions of Benjamin Franklin and the Junto to Adult Education: A Dialectical Approach." Unpublished doctoral dissertation, Department of Leadership and Educational Policy Studies, Northern Illinois University, 1988.

Ilsley, P. J. *Enhancing the Volunteer Experience: New Insights on Strengthening Volunteer Participation, Learning, and Commitment.* San Francisco: Jossey-Bass, 1990.

Lindeman, E. C. *The Meaning of Adult Education.* Montreal, Quebec, Canada: Harvest House, 1961. (Originally published 1926.)

Morris, R. C. *Reading, 'Riting, and Reconstruction: The Education of Freedmen in the South, 1861–1870.* Chicago: University of Chicago Press, 1981.

Peterson, E. "A Phenomenological Investigation of Self-Will and Its Relation to Successes in African American Women." Unpublished doctoral dissertation, Department of Leadership and Educational Policy Studies, Northern Illinois University, 1991.

Rachal, J. R. "Freedom's Crucible: William T. Richardson and the Schooling of the Freedmen." *Adult Education Quarterly,* 1986, 37 (1), 14–22.

Schied, F. M. "Towards a Reconceptualization of the Historical Foundations of Adult Education: The Contributions of Radical German Americans to Workers' Education." Unpublished doctoral dissertation, Department of Leadership and Educational Policy Studies, Northern Illinois University, 1991.

Tough, A. *Crucial Questions About the Future.* Lanham, Md.: Unipub, 1991.

Welton, M. "On the Eve of a Great Mass Movement: Reflections on the Origins of the Canadian Association of Adult Education." In F. Cassidy and R. Faris (eds.), *Choosing Our Future.* Toronto, Canada: Ontario Institute for Studies in Education, 1987.

Zacharakis-Jutz, J. "Straight to the Heart of a Union, Straight to the Heart of a Movement: Workers' Education in the WPWA Between 1951 and 1953." Unpublished doctoral dissertation, Department of Leadership and Educational Policy Studies, Northern Illinois University, 1991.

PAUL J. ILSLEY is associate professor of adult education at Northern Illinois University, De Kalb.

PART TWO

Should Adult and
Continuing Education
Strive for Professionalization?

The drive to professionalize undermines the moral force and
emancipatory intent of adult and continuing education.

Adult and Continuing Education Should Resist Further Professionalization

Michael Collins

In this chapter on the issue of professionalization, I begin with a critically oriented statement of my position. The personal commentary that then follows is intended to explain how I arrived at the conviction that in the quest for professionalization we lose the meaning of adult education (Lindeman, [1926] 1961).

Critical Prelude

My opposition to professionalization does not mean that I have no concern about the achievement of competent performance. We need expertise and experts. However, I have become convinced that undue emphasis on professionalization actually restricts our best efforts to become better at our work. For adult educators, the process of becoming better at our work means helping others do the same. On these claims, there is consensus among all thoughtful opponents of the professionalization trend in adult and continuing education. Resistance to professionalization does not stem from a cavalier disregard for doing the job well. As an adult educator, I encourage others to take charge of their own work. But I recognize that the attendant commitment does not emerge from the bureaucratic stipulations of the professionalization paradigm. My stance is in line with the ethical intent behind such notions as learning how to learn and education for empowerment, which adult educators tend to espouse.

Clearly, I have no problem with the sentiments invoked when the terms *professionalism* or *professional* are used to convey appreciation for skillful performance of a task. Since we need expertise (although it is part

NEW DIRECTIONS FOR ADULT AND CONTINUING EDUCATION, no. 54, Summer 1992 © Jossey-Bass Publishers

of my thesis that the cult of professionalism creates overdependence on designated experts), I think that adult education must be concerned with the design of relevant training. My concern is with the paraphernalia of credentialing, licensing, certification, and other regulatory procedures associated with the professionalization phenomenon. These essential trappings of established professions have more to do with exercise of control and establishment of a monopolistic practice than with guarantees of competent performance.

It is true that the earning of certificates and the granting of licenses are usually accompanied by formal requirements to demonstrate competence (although this is not always the case), but demonstration of competent performance does not have to rely on this type of evidence. Nor does this evidence guarantee competent performance. One could readily agree with these observations and still point out that a certificate is a useful formal indicator of the training that an individual has received. I think that this is a reasonable position to take. But when we consider the entire apparatus of certification, licensing, credentialing, and mandatory continuing education deployed in the maintenance of professionalized fields of practice, it becomes apparent that professionalization is primarily about exercising exclusive authority over designated areas of practical knowledge.

The accumulation and protection of professionalized knowledge ensure that those who have privileged access to it are able to make a good living as members of the middle class. Few will want to argue with the concern to guarantee a reasonable living for skillful practitioners. However, I think that adult educators in particular need to question the aspirations of professions to control the availability and nature of expertise.

Illich's work (1970, 1977) on the disabling effects of professionalization within modern society is of paramount importance for adult educators. Despite his utopian tendencies, there is a potent moral force to Illich's analysis. He provides a powerful account of how the cult of professionalization shapes our institutions, distorts learning processes, and infantilizes us all. Illich's theorizing lacks an adequate political agenda, but his insights are supported by important feminist perspectives that, for example, highlight the prevailing patriarchal makeup of established professions. In an important addition to feminist scholarship, Witz (1991) shows how male power organized through the professions limits the employment aspirations of women.

An adequate account of the culture and history of professionalization, though very relevant, is beyond the scope of this chapter. Fortunately, there are many well-written texts on the development and nature of modern professions. Some useful sources for adult educators include Bledstein (1978), Larson (1977), Jackson (1970), and Friedson (1986). A careful reading of these sources reveals how professions, and their claim for special privileges, have been developed and established in modern capitalist societies. I draw on works such as these to support my view that even if we ignore ethical arguments against professionalizing adult and continuing education, objective circumstances do not favor initiatives to professionalize our very diversified field of practice. Accordingly, we should abandon any pretensions about professionalizing adult education and occupy ourselves with the practical concerns of a vocation that can play an important role in today's society.

Personal Encounters

As a doctoral student, I attended my first Adult Education Association of the U.S.A. conference in 1977. The late J. Roby Kidd, an eminent Canadian adult educator, was keynote speaker. He expressed deep disappointment at the way that adult educators who embraced mandatory continuing education were so "pathetically pleased to be wanted" by the professions. Along with many others who were active at that conference in forming a National Association for Voluntary Learning, I was heartened by Roby Kidd's position on this issue.

During the months prior to the conference, in the early stages of my graduate education at Northern Illinois University in De Kalb, I had been particularly impressed with the commitment, competence, and friendliness of faculty and graduate students, all of whom were experienced practitioners. What was not in keeping with this perception was what I saw as an undue deference to technique, including formalized measures of accountability, among many of us. This dependence on artificial notions of "objectivity" did not jibe with the careful, practical pedagogy that I witnessed within the program and in its work with the wider field of practice. My experience of contradictions between commitment to practical performance and an obsession with technique for its own sake was shared by others. My reaction was not due solely to the fact that I was a foreign student. Subsequently, I came to realize that the enthronement of formal needs assessment instruments, predetermined steps for program development, standardized learning packages, formulaic learning contracts, and positivistic (statistical-empirical) research methods had a purpose beyond ensuring competent performance. They were very important signifiers of specialized expertise—the trappings of professionalization. It was reasonable, from the prevalent view of modern adult education practice, to muster them in support of coercive initiatives such as mandatory continuing education under the rubric of lifelong learning. The professionalizers had led us into other-directed and self-directed learning.

My concerns about the prevalence of technocratic approaches in adult education, and what they augured in terms of the quest for professionalization, did not stem from a whimsical distaste for well-organized practice. As a graduate in business and economics and a former track athlete, I recognized the need for efficiency and appropriate standards. The career in business systems in which I embarked after earning my first degree was consistent with this viewpoint. When I eventually made the move into teaching and adult education (gradually and with a great deal of thought because it meant abandoning a potentially very lucrative career in business), it was with an intention of bringing my business training to a field of practice that fell short in its concern for relevant standards and competent performance. These earlier thoughts were rather grandiose, I now realize, but in keeping with the tiresome rhetoric about the need for accountability, efficiency, and competition in education that has been elevated beyond all reason in recent years.

Prior to entering a doctoral program, I was head of commerce in a Canadian secondary school and district coordinator of adult education. The practical challenges of the adult education program commanded more of my attention than did an imperative to redesign a twelfth-grade office machines course, which would have become redundant before I even started. I realized then the futility of pretending that public education can provide the up-to-date equipment and hands-on training available in business and industry. Mention of this insight is relevant here because I see the same mistake being made in modern adult education practice under such professionalized categories as human resources development and competence-based education.

Along the way to entering a doctoral program in adult and continuing education, I had completed a master's degree on a part-time basis. During my thesis research, I began to understand that adult education in its institutional form has been a context for conflicting interests from the outset. My research focus was the mechanics' institutes of early nineteenth-century England from which emerged a widespread institutionalized movement in adult education. The key figure in founding the mechanics' institutes, Thomas Hodgskin, had envisioned an adult education movement that would advance the practical and emancipatory interests of working-class people. His hopes were soon dashed by the largely well-meaning interventions of middle-class patrons, representatives of the burgeoning business and professional interests of early nineteenth-century England. They ensured that working-class educational needs were defined according to middle-class values. From my present perspective, I now recognize that the mechanics' institutes prefigured modern adult education practice.

I wrote an article (Collins, 1972) showing how the mechanics' institutes had failed to come anywhere near Thomas Hodgskin's aspirations for "the education of a free people" (Halevay, 1956, p. 87). My article appeared in the same issue of *Adult Education: Journal of Research and Theory* as Lloyd's (1972) introductory essay on the pedagogical work of Paulo Freire. For me, the joint appearance of these articles was particularly fortuitous. Hodgskin, like Freire, was a political theorist as well as an outstanding adult educator with a clear-cut commitment to the education of ordinary working people. For Hodgskin and Freire, a preoccupation with the professionalization of adult education would be absurd. Contemporary professionalized discourse about ethics and adult education (as in "ethics and the law" or "ethics and medicine") is arrant nonsense for those who, like Hodgskin and Freire, recognize that ethical and political commitment resides at the core of adult education practice.

In my subsequent academic work, I have been largely concerned with a critical analysis of the technocratic tendency in modern adult education, which characterizes its quest for professionalization. At a theoretical level, my work has been guided by phenomenological investigations, hermeneutics, and critical theory. Through these theoretical perspectives, it is possible to reveal the epistemological shortcomings and coercive consequences of pedagogical innovations that typify technocratic rationality in adult education and to describe alternative approaches for the achievement of competent performance (Collins, 1987). I argue that relevant alternatives to the technocratic rationality that sustains the quest for professionalization in our field necessitate a commitment to adult education as a vocation (Collins, 1991). Otherwise the pedagogical artifacts of modern adult education (prepackaged competence-based education, formulaic needs assessment instruments, functionalist evaluation procedures, learning contracts, and so on) will continue to thwart prospects for genuine emancipatory pedagogy.

Implications for Practice

A growing number of adult educators are becoming critical of the professionalized pedagogical strategies highlighted here, even when these are presented under the banner of self-directed learning. However, the recent "critical turn" in adult education has been followed by some who, while recognizing that critical discourse is now in vogue, do not fully appreciate its practical and political intent. They seem to think that it can be incorporated within the comfortable bailiwick of professionalized practice. Our response to the homogenization of critical thought by the professionalizers should be to pose ethical and political problems that emanate from involvement with critical theory in adult education: "Now that we understand, what should we do?" In the light of our critical discourse, we have to decide whose interests we serve and which side of the fence we are on with regard to the critical issues of our times. Some adult educators find this stance overly divisive. Professionalized practice is concerned with consensus formation and seeks to avoid consideration of contentious issues in ways that could undermine carefully established authoritative parameters. To counter this apolitical professionalizing tendency, we need to incorporate a questioning of all authoritative, professionalized assumptions into our pedagogy. Adult education curriculum should be constructed with a view toward reducing the present overdependence on professionals.

The recent critical turn in adult education, if followed, should steer us decisively away from the professionalizing aspirations of modern adult education practice and toward the committed pedagogy of Thomas Hodgskin and Paulo Freire. The pedagogy of the oppressed (Freire, 1974)—education for ordinary men and women—places emancipatory interests above technical rationality. From Freire we learn that an emancipatory pedagogy entails the use of techniques relevantly identified in a local context, "tools for conviviality" to use Illich's (1970) expression, and the formation of curriculum from students' reports on their everyday lives. The process involves educators in an egalitarian relationship with students, where a concern for personal development is accompanied by recognition of the need for political involvement. This pedagogical orientation contrasts markedly with a professionalized elite's aspirations toward objective detachment.

Even adult educators who are skeptical about prospects for an emancipatory pedagogy should realize that professionalization does not offer a sensible option. At a time when the monopolistic privileges of professionalized medicine and law are coming under scrutiny, it is very unlikely that a diverse field such as adult education can achieve professionalized status. Why waste time trying to go in that direction?

Clearly, we should be concerned about the creation of secure jobs for adult educators and improving the conditions of our work. For these purposes, some form of organization is needed. While it is not feasible to think in terms of one big union for adult educators, the trade union form of organization should be favored by adult educators at this time. In some institutions, adult educators are already organized within employees' associations. Where this is not an option, it would be advantageous for adult educators to join with appropriate workers' organizations in their localities. We are workers after all.

Instead of wrapping our work in the cloak of professionalization, we can align our pedagogical commitments and curriculum more relevantly with the struggles of ordinary men and women for whom the privileges of professionalized status are beyond reach. Analysis of the status of modern adult education practice inevitably leads to the conclusion that ambitions toward further professionalization of the field are both pretentious and dysfunctional. Are we so pathetically eager to be recognized by established professions?

References

Bledstein, B. J. *The Culture of Professionalism.* New York: Norton, 1978.
Collins, M. "The Mechanics' Institutes—Education for the Working Man?" *Adult Education: Journal of Research and Theory,* 1972, 23 (1), 37–47.

Collins, M. *Competence in Adult Education: A New Perspective.* Lanham, Md.: Unipub, 1987.

Collins, M. *Adult Education as Vocation.* New York: Routledge & Kegan Paul, 1991.

Freire, P. *Pedagogy of the Oppressed.* New York: Seabury, 1974.

Friedson, E. *Professional Powers.* Chicago: University of Chicago Press, 1986.

Halevay, E. *Thomas Hodgskin.* London, England: Ernest Benn, 1956.

Illich, I. *De-Schooling Society.* New York: HarperCollins, 1970.

Illich, I. (ed.). *Disabling Professions.* London, England: Marion Boyars, 1977.

Jackson, J. A. (ed.). *Professions and Professionalization.* Cambridge, England: Cambridge University Press, 1970.

Larson, M. S. *The Rise of Professionalism: A Sociological Analysis.* Berkeley and Los Angeles: University of California Press, 1977.

Lindeman, E. C. *The Meaning of Adult Education.* Montreal, Quebec, Canada: Harvest House, 1961. (Originally published 1926.)

Lloyd, A. "Freire, Conscientization, and Adult Education." *Adult Education: Journal of Research and Theory,* 1972, 23 (1), 3–20.

Witz, A. *Professions and Patriarchy.* New York: Routledge & Kegan Paul, 1991.

MICHAEL COLLINS is professor of adult and continuing education at the University of Saskatchewan, Saskatoon, Saskatchewan, Canada.

*The field should accept the process of professionalization and deal
with the options available in shaping the meaning and outcome
of this process for practice.*

Adult and Continuing Education Should Strive for Professionalization

Ronald M. Cervero

There are many ways to think about professionalization (Cervero, 1988).
Before proceeding too far, then, let me offer a note about what I am not
talking about. I am not referring to how *professional* an individual is. In
common parlance, this term has come to mean a competent, committed
worker. Thus, we speak of professional car mechanics, plumbers, and exter-
minators. If this were the definition, adult educators would already be as
professional as the members of any other occupation. My unit of analysis
must be the occupation rather than the individual because individuals do
not professionalize but occupations do.

In this chapter, I use a socioeconomic definition of professionalization
from the sociological literature. Larson (1977) says that professionalization
is the process by which producers of special services constitute and control
the market for their services. For this professional market to exist, a distinctive commodity must be produced. Now, professional work is only a fictitious
commodity. Unlike industrial labor, most professions produce intangible
goods in that their products are inextricably bound to the persons who produce them. It follows, then, that the producers themselves have to be produced if their products are to be given a distinctive form. In other words,
professionals must be adequately trained and socialized so as to provide recognizably distinct services for exchange on the professional market.

At this point, it is useful to examine in greater detail the one condition
that has been a necessary step in the professionalization of every occupation. In order to provide a recognizably distinct service, a profession must
have a recognizably distinct and standardized knowledge base that is taught
to its new members. For most professions, the production of knowledge

and the production of practitioners are united into the same structure. That is, the model of research and training institutionalized by the modern university gives to professions the means of controlling their knowledge bases as well as of awarding credentials certifying that the practitioner possesses this recognizably distinct type of knowledge. Therefore, the level of professionalization of an occupation can be assessed by the extent to which its credentials are accepted as necessary to provide a specific type of service.

Using this definition of professionalization, we can assess the extent to which various subfields of adult education have professionalized. Not unexpectedly, the most professionalized subfield is the professoriate, with a reasonable estimate being that at least 80 percent of the Commission of Professors of Adult Education have earned doctorates in the field. In examining other subfields, however, the levels of professionalization drop dramatically. For example, 94 percent of the teachers in Adult Basic Education (ABE) are certified to teach elementary or secondary education, while only 13 percent of ABE teachers are certified in adult education (Development Associates, 1980). The situation in continuing higher education is only slightly better. Sixty-eight percent of deans and directors have doctorates. Of these, only 25 percent earned their degrees in adult education (Azzaretto, 1986). I expect that a similar situation exists in most, if not all, subfields in adult education. Except for the professoriate, I would conclude that adult educators have not managed to constitute and control the market for their services in any subfield of practice.

While the question of professionalization is interesting to debate in the abstract, it is nearly a nonissue as a practical matter. In fact, I truly believe that the normative question about future professionalization of adult education is hardly worth discussing. Unless all graduate programs in adult education are dismantled, adult educators will continue their efforts to constitute and control the market for their services by producing certified adult educators. The process of professionalization began nearly sixty years ago with the establishment of degree programs in universities. This process is a function of pervasive social, political, and economic forces inherent to Anglo-American capitalist societies (Friedson, 1986; Larson, 1977). While we certainly have options as individuals about whether to participate in this process, it is difficult to imagine what other alternatives we have as an occupation. Let us accept our involvement in the process of professionalization and move to the more important issue concerning our options in shaping the professionalization of the field.

How I Arrived at My Position on Professionalization

I arrived at my position primarily through my experience as a faculty member in adult education graduate programs for the past twelve years and my work in continuing education for the professions during that same period of time. These experiences have demonstrated to me that while members of a profession may receive common training, they use this common background for very different personal and social purposes. The assumption that professions are best understood as communities united by common interests is simply a myth. Just as in *any* other occupation, we see graduates of adult education degree programs serving very different social ends. These range from working as advocates in progressive social movements to working as educators in the military. Thus, I have not devoted my efforts to get adult education out of the professionalization process. Rather, I have focused on ways to open up spaces for individuals with very different social agendas in graduate programs and in my own practice as an adult educator.

This interchange between Collins (this volume) and me is only the most recent example of the historical debate over whether the field should seek to professionalize (Griffith, 1980). For those who have argued against accepting the dominant models, an attractive alternative has been to suggest the need to find or create different models of professionalization. Carlson (1977, pp. 60-61) has stated this option most directly: "Are there any viable alternatives to the traditional type of professionalization? . . . A careful search for alternative approaches to professionalization is one of the most important . . . research areas in the field." I agree with Carlson and have come to my position through work with many other professions and after an extensive examination of the literature in preparation for writing my book *Effective Continuing Education for Professionals* (Cervero, 1988).

I found that new models of professionalization are being discussed in many other professions. Schön (1983) argues for a new kind of professional, the "reflective practitioner." Carroll (1985, p. 43), in considering the question of professionalization in relation to the ministry, answered by saying that it is necessary to "reconceive and reinterpret the professional model to make it more applicable to ordained ministry." Giroux and McLaren (1986) argue for a reconceptualization of the teaching profession to revive the values of democratic citizenship and social justice. Finally, Kissam (1986, p. 323) sees in the decline of law school professionalism the opportunity to "reduce the concepts of legal formalism and legal autonomy to their appropriate, limited place in legal education, and to replace these concepts with a more contextual and more critical study of the legal process." Thus, we see adult education facing many of the same issues as other, more established professions.

The major unanswered question, however, concerns what alternate professional models might look like. I believe that we have simply not known where to look. We have been busy arguing against professionalization as if this were going to create new models. It will not. Rather than focus on the process by which adult educators are certified, we need to focus on how adult educators use their power and to what ends. My work with and study about the professions shows that they are not homogeneous communities with shared sets of values working toward common ends. Professions are characterized more accurately as "loose amalgamations of segments pursuing different objectives and more or less held together under a common name at a particular period of history" (Bucher and Strauss, 1961, p. 326).

This approach forces us to shift our attention away from what professionals have in common as a result of the professionalization process, such as education, status, and knowledge, to how they use these common characteristics for different social purposes. For example, some clergy see their function only as ensuring the personal salvation of the members of their congregation. In contrast, others such as those working out of the tradition of liberation theology, define their role as improving the material condition of people's lives. Some physicians are refusing to serve the poor and elderly because changes in third-party payment systems have limited the amounts of reimbursement under Medicare and Medicaid. On the other hand, some physicians operate free clinics for these groups. The back-to-basics movement calls for a restructuring of schools to raise the level of literacy necessary to meet the requirements of a high-technology economy. Instead of upholding the social order, as these changes would do, many call for teachers and administrators to develop a "critical pedagogy" (Greene, 1986).

These examples show that we do not need to create alternate models out of thin air. Graduates of adult education degree programs show this same diversity in the ends to which they put their knowledge and skill. By looking at the practices of adult education rather than the process of training, we already have many alternate models of professionalization.

Improving Practice

It is my hope that the field can move beyond the issue of whether it should professionalize. Adult education has answered this question by engaging in the process of awarding credentials through higher education institutions. Instead, attention should be focused on the issue of which models of professionalization should be followed. Professionalization should recognize that different (and to some extent competing) purposes, knowledge, and ideologies underlie the work of adult educators. The very least we can do is ensure that these differences are represented in the content of graduate training programs and in the constituencies of professional associations. We must not trivialize the knowledge and practice of those who work outside the mainstream. We must recognize that adult educators' work with marginalized members of society, such as the poor and racial minorities, is as valid as that of educators who focus on dominant groups, such as business and the professions.

In closing, I offer my own vision of the framework of professionalization that the field should follow. I believe that the following six principles can effectively guide the field along the path to professionalization.

First, adult educators are not values-neutral possessors of a technical process. We are political actors within a social structure, and our programs always have outcomes that either maintain this structure or change it. We must continually review and reassess the ends of our practice, not just the means.

Second, adult educators must recognize that problems that require learning usually do not develop within the individual but rather are a function of the individual within the social-political-economic environment. Thus, individuals and their learning needs cannot be isolated from the circumstances that produced those needs. Further, we must be careful to discriminate between problems for which education is the appropriate solution and those for which it is not.

Third, the larger portion of adults' learning does not require assistance. Adult educators should not seek to destroy the beauty of friends teaching friends. Rather, we must discriminate among situations where assistance would provide more effective learning and where it would not. That is, professional adult education is not necessarily better than nonprofessional adult education.

Fourth, educators should not seek autonomy in decision making regarding learners' needs or the solutions to those needs. Rather, learners should be involved, both individually and collectively, in determining both needs and solutions.

Fifth, learning needs should not be treated as deficiencies of the individual that can be treated and remedied. Rather, learning needs should be viewed as an adult's right to know. That is, the vision of adult education should be revised from a medical model to a human rights model.

Sixth, educators have a symbiotic relationship with adult learners. While the learners could probably survive without the educators, the educators cannot survive without the learners. Thus, the temptation to create and exploit learning needs to further the needs of adult education must be avoided.

Professionalization can be a force for good in society. I believe that if these principles guide the process of professionalization, the field will value the meaning and the outcome of this process for practice. Without a progressive set of principles guiding the process, professionalization will serve only as a mechanism for the creation and protection of jobs for adult educators. We have a choice about the meaning and outcome of this process for our field. Let us stand together and make the right choices.

References

Azzaretto, J. F. "Survey Results of Continuing Educators for the Professions." Paper presented at the National University Continuing Education Association Conference, Portland, Oregon, April 1986.

Bucher, R., and Strauss, A. "Professions in Process." *American Journal of Sociology*, 1961, *66*, 325–334.

Carlson, R. A. "Professionalization of Adult Education: An Historical-Philosophical Analysis." *Adult Education*, 1977, *28* (1), 53–63.

Carroll, J. W. "The Professional Model of Ministry—Is It Worth Saving?" *Theological Education*, 1985, *21* (2), 7–48.

Cervero, R. M. *Effective Continuing Education for Professionals.* San Francisco: Jossey-Bass, 1988.

Development Associates. *An Assessment of the State-Administered Programs of the Adult Education Act.* Washington, D.C.: Government Printing Office, 1980.

Friedson, E. *Professional Powers.* Chicago: University of Chicago Press, 1986.

Giroux, H. A., and McLaren, P. "Teacher Education and the Politics of Engagement: The Case for Democratic Schooling." *Harvard Educational Review*, 1986, *56* (3), 213–238.

Greene, M. "In Search of a Critical Pedagogy." *Harvard Educational Review*, 1986, *56* (4), 427–441.

Griffith, W. S. "Personnel Preparation: Is There a Continuing Education Profession?" In H. A. Alford (ed.), *Power and Conflict in Continuing Education.* Belmont, Calif.: Wadsworth, 1980.

Kissam, P. C. "The Decline of Law School Professionalism." *University of Pennsylvania Law Review*, 1986, *134* (2), 251–324.

Larson, M. S. *The Rise of Professionalism: A Sociological Analysis.* Berkeley and Los Angeles: University of California Press, 1977.

Schön, D. A. *The Reflective Practitioner.* New York: Basic Books, 1983.

RONALD M. CERVERO is a professor in the Department of Adult Education, University of Georgia, Athens. He has been a member of the executive committee of the Commission of Professors of Adult Education and is currently the co-editor of Adult Education Quarterly.

PART THREE

Where Should Leaders in
Adult and Continuing Education
Come from?

Leaders drawn from more diverse disciplines will bring different perspectives, understanding, and enrichment to the field of adult and continuing education.

Leaders of Adult and Continuing Education Should Come from Outside the Field

Peter Jarvis

Who are the leaders in the field? Are they the managers, the policymakers, or the academics who teach and write about it? Leadership is a problematic concept, but I assume that leaders occupy positions of influence and power in adult and continuing education, and that they may perform any combination of the above roles since these areas are not functionally discrete.

What is the field of adult and continuing education? Adults are educated in many different areas, at work, in their leisure, and so on. Where, then, is adult and continuing education? And who are adult educators? They are individuals who perform certain functions: policy-making, managing, and teaching in adult and continuing education. Hence, one way to identify our complex field is to suggest that wherever these functions are performed in the process of teaching and learning with adults, there is adult and continuing education. In this sense, adult education is a very wide field of practice, which can occur in almost any sector of society.

However, these answers do not completely cover all of the above questions because there is also a sector of society defined as adult and continuing education. It is embodied in the structures of society, often funded and administered by central agencies. It constitutes a much more narrow, taken-for-granted conception of the field, and it is often this conception, the structural field, that is studied in university graduate programs. Hence, we are left with two approaches to understanding the field: (1) a structural approach, narrowly contained by those structures defined in society at large as adult and continuing education, and (2) a functional approach, broadly including every part of society where the functions of teaching and learning are performed among adults.

I adopt here the functional approach to the field, perhaps because I have not come into the field by the traditional route of studying for a university doctorate in adult and continuing education. Consequently, I conclude that many of the leaders, or potential leaders, in the field should be drawn from a broad pool of candidates. The very nature of a broad perspective on the field of adult education implies that there should be at least three sources other than the traditional route into leadership through university doctoral programs: from areas in the functional field that are excluded from the structural one; from the whole of the field of education; from other disciplines that provide significant ways of understanding the education of adults.

Leaders from the Functional Field of Adult Education

In the opening discussion, I suggested that the education of adults is both about function and structure: The latter defines a narrow perspective, whereas the former spans a variety of sectors of society. Let me illustrate this functional approach in another profession, medicine, although examples could easily be drawn from numerous other professions. Medical educators are involved in the education of adults, although many of them might not identify themselves as members of the adult education profession, nor might they study for an Ed.D. However, in their educational work they may evolve tremendously insightful understanding about the education of adults. They might develop their own theories about education and even conduct their own research on it. That research would most likely be published in medical journals rather than in adult educational materials, since medical educators identify with medically oriented publications. The research might be developed into sophisticated educational theory but remain unknown to the structural field of adult and continuing education. A whole body of this theory might have already emerged, or be in the process of developing, in another profession, such as social work or nursing.

A personal experience is also illustrative. I was speaking at a one-day regional nursing education conference in 1991, and a graduate student who was studying with me at that time, a school teacher educator, came to the conference. At the end of the day, she spoke to the assembled gathering of nurse educators, telling them that she wished that the level of educational debate in the school teacher education department in which she worked was as sophisticated as the debate in which she had participated on that day. This is but one example, but it indicates that there are growing bodies of theory and practice about the education of adults that do not normally find their way into the more narrow understanding of our field. In much the same way that many adult educators have come into the structural field of adult education from agricultural extension, it seems just as logical to expect that educators from other areas of our wide field might be regarded as a part of it and contribute to its leadership.

Leaders from the Field of Education

The suggestion that some of our leaders might come from school teacher education might be regarded as quite contentious, as some of the recent debates in the Commission of Professors of Adult Education in North America about professional standards and the recent publication of a code of standards indicate. But if we claim that educators of adults, in whatever field of education they function, should be counted within our ranks, it seems rather illogical not to be prepared to draw into our field those whose work is also in the field of education, albeit the education of school children. We all work in education, we are all concerned about the processes of teaching and learning, and so why should we not be prepared to draw some of our leaders from this branch of the field of education?

Not only are we all concerned about similar processes, we have common founding theorists, such as Dewey (1916, 1938). The insights of scholars and administrators who have worked in elementary school education could enrich our understanding of education, just as much as the recent studies in the education of adults could enhance the study of the education of children. Educators of children are beginning to recognize that there is not a large divide between the education of children and adults. At a recent meeting of the European Association of Research into Learning and Instruction—an organization primarily of school teacher educators with backgrounds in psychology—an adult education special interest group was formed, and one of the invited speakers at that conference was an adult educator.

Perhaps now is the time to recognize that educators of children and educators of adults have a lot in common and that we could benefit each other if we would share more rather than seek to draw laborious and even false distinctions between andragogy and pedagogy. Therefore, the practice of drawing some of the leaders in our field from the education of children could help us all create a body of educational knowledge relevant to all educators, regardless of where and whom they teach. After all, we are all engaged in education, and the development of a body of knowledge about lifelong education must be the aim of all of us!

Leaders from Other Disciplines

If the education of adults is a functional field of practice, then its study is even more specialized. Each single field of practice, whether medical education, nursing education, or the education of adults in community colleges, can be studied from a variety of perspectives. Three perspectives in particular are of interest here: the practical, knowledge of the practical (or practical knowledge), and knowledge about the practical. Clearly, this is part of the theory-practice problem, which has been discussed in detail by Cervero (1991). However, my approach is slightly different from his.

The Practical. The practical perspective refers to the fact that practitioners learn in practice, and the knowledge and skills that they learn are based on the pragmatic assumption that they can achieve their aims and objectives through what they do. This assumption is common among other educators performing in different educational fields of practice, since this makes us a functional profession.

Knowledge of the Practical. Knowledge of practice is the practical knowledge that is specific to the field of practice being undertaken. This knowledge is a combination of the "how-to-do," which is discovered in practice itself, and the "knowledge-how-to-do." However, this latter knowledge is also another combination: It is the general "knowledge-how" that is applicable to all education of adults, but it is also that relevant "knowledge-how" that refers to the specific knowledge base of the practice in question, for example, medicinal education and community development. Hence, knowledge of practice is both functional and structural.

Knowledge About the Practical. Knowledge about practice is the knowledge that students from the academic disciplines develop about our field of practice. For instance, a sociologist may specialize in the study of nursing education, or a philosopher in liberal adult education. The former might write an insightful sociology of nursing education, and the latter a perceptive philosophical analysis of liberal adult education. Traditionally, philosophy and the social sciences have comprised the foundation disciplines, even though Jensen, Liveright, and Hallenbeck (1964) wrote of borrowing from the disciplines. It is my contention that neither of these approaches is correct. For instance, practical educational knowledge, as described above, is an integrated body of applied knowledge that, if broken down into the disciplines, might be categorized as a unique constellation of bits of different applied disciplines. But this breakdown is never done, nor should it be, because this is not the way that practical knowledge arises. It is practical knowledge sui generis, so that practical educational knowledge is based on practice not on the disciplines, and this is the foundation of practice. Practical knowledge is driven by practice alone. We do not borrow from the disciplines in order to generate it or even to teach it.

This characterization of knowledge about practice does not preclude the sociologist or the philosopher, or any members of any other disciplines, from studying the fields of practice within the education of adults. Now, these studies are uniquely philosophical, sociological, and so on. They are driven by the demands of the discipline and not by the demands of the practice. Educational knowledge is practical knowledge, not an academic discipline knowledge: We can have a sociology of education but it is nonsense to talk of an education of sociology, or an adult education of philosophy. The education of adults is a subject that can be taught, but its epistemological basis is profoundly different in nature from that of the academic disciplines (Jarvis, 1991).

If academic sociologists, philosophers, and so on study our field and develop unique insights that can help us better understand ourselves and our place in society, then we should not be ignorant of their work or of its significance. Indeed, if we are unaware of the relevance of their analyses, then that is an even greater reason why we should adopt a broader approach. If their work is useful, then it would benefit us to have them in our midst and to have their leadership enrich our field. Hence, it would be wise to reach even beyond the functional field and to draw some of our leaders from this wider arena.

Conclusion

The gist of my position is simple: The functional field of adult and continuing education is complex, but the traditional university program, which is the normal route to leadership in our field, tends to reflect a narrow, structural understanding. If we continue to reproduce this narrow perspective, we shall, in effect, continue to move away from mainstream academic and policy debates and hence continue to impoverish our field. But by having more leaders who are conversant with these debates, we can help make our field more mainstream. If these leaders are drawn from the wider field, they will bring different perspectives and understandings that can only enrich our field.

The suggestion here is not that people who move into our field from elsewhere should be foisted upon us by university authorities seeking to off-load surplus staff. Rather, we should be prepared to open up leadership roles, first, to people from other areas who are fully conversant in the complexities and richness of our field. To assume a leadership role in ignorance is unprofessional. To allow such leaders in our field would be to neglect our own professional duty and understanding.

References

Cervero, R. M. "Changing Relationships Between Theory and Practice." In J. M. Peters and P. Jarvis (eds.), *Adult Education: Evolution and Achievements in a Developing Field of Study.* San Francisco: Jossey-Bass, 1991.

Dewey, J. *Democracy and Education.* New York: Free Press, 1916.

Dewey, J. *Experience and Education.* New York: Collier Books, 1938.

Jarvis, P. "Practical Knowledge and Theoretical Analyses in Adult and Continuing Education." In M. Friedenthal-Hasse and others (eds.), *Erwachsenenbildung in Kontext* [Adult education in context]. Bad Heilbronn, Germany: Klinkhardt, 1991.

Jensen, G., Liveright, A. A., and Hallenbeck, W. (eds.). *Adult Education: Outlines of an Emerging Field of University Study.* Washington, D.C.: Adult Education Association of the U.S.A., 1964.

PETER JARVIS is reader in the Department of Educational Studies, University of Surrey, Guildford, Surrey, England.

*A romantic interpretation of the history of adult education has led
to a false impression of the most appropriate source of leaders for
the twenty-first century. Serious reflection on the evolution of the
field leads to the conclusion that tomorrow's leaders for the field
should come from within.*

Adult and Continuing Education Leaders Should Come from Within the Field

William S. Griffith

I am convinced that if we in adult education look for leadership outside
our profession, we shall remain unable to develop sufficient full-time professional positions and career ladders needed to efficiently and effectively
provide appropriate adult learning opportunities for all. I believe that
dependence on the imported leader whose vision of adult education is
limited to one discipline, one clientele, one content, one medium, or one
set of objectives prevents the sound development of our field. This conclusion is based on thirty-nine years of experience in practical as well as
academic adult education, including extensive involvement with the American Association for Adult and Continuing Education (AAACE) and the
Adult Education Association of the U.S.A. (AEA/USA) at the local, state,
provincial, regional, national, and international levels.

   In this chapter, I explain why I have reached this conclusion. I review
a critical distinction, describe aspects of our field of practice, identify
problems encountered in building on ideas and leaders from other areas,
and conclude by noting the importance of changing conditions to the type
of leaders required for the twenty-first century.

Educators of Adults Versus Adult Educators

Educators of adults are distinct from adult educators, and the distinction
has important implications. The former have narrowly focused goals that
typically address problems in a single sector of the field. The latter have

broad aspirations for the entire field. Educators of adults have mainly practical concerns, narrower visions, and limited ambitions and typically address single programmatic issues through adult education. In contrast, adult educators have a high regard for professionalism, specialized academic preparation for their work, and a concern for strengthening the financial base of the entire field (Griffith, 1989). A recognition of this distinction is critical for clear thinking about leadership in our field.

Problem of Amateur Adult Education Administration

The improvement of adult education leadership is hindered because many adult education administrators have not had the benefit of graduate study in their field of application and fail to appreciate its value. A study conducted by the National University Continuing Education Association (1989) revealed that almost 100 percent of the responding deans and directors of university extension divisions had worked in other fields prior to assuming their administrative leadership roles. Only slightly more than half of them said that adult education was their career goal. To complicate matters further, when they were asked to rank the usefulness of degrees in various fields in terms of preparation for an administrative role in adult education, fewer than half of them considered degrees in adult and continuing education to be very useful!

So, if many of those who are holding full-time administrative positions have come to them through the back door, and if they are not inclined to seek out staff members educationally prepared in adult education, it should not be surprising that they would not favor further development of adult education as a profession. Unwittingly, they retard its further development, first, by denying any claim to professional status and, second, by hiring staff members with no greater grounding in adult education than they themselves have. Yet, university graduate study in the field has existed for nearly sixty years.

Establishment of Graduate Study Programs

Cyril Houle, doyen of American adult education scholars, noted nearly thirty years ago that, historically, the leaders of the field acquired their knowledge and skills through an apprenticeship or through trial and error (Houle, 1964). Twenty-five years later, Judith Koloski, former executive director of AAACE, noted that "only a small number of the individuals responsible for the policy development, management, administration, or teaching and counseling of individuals enrolled in [adult education] programs have been trained as adult educators" (Koloski, 1989, p. 72). Whereas adult educators have not been employed to serve in leadership roles, educators of adults have been eager to move in and understandably defend their own lack of graduate preparation for their positions.

Acknowledgment that the creative pioneers did not have the advantage of graduate study in their chosen field is not to advocate that graduate study is therefore unnecessary, any more than it would be reasonable to assert that since some people manage to earn above-average incomes without having become literate, literacy skills are superfluous. Through 1991, at least four thousand individuals had invested their time, money, and energy in the successful pursuit of doctoral degrees in adult education. At least twenty thousand others have earned magistral degrees in this field. Thus, there is a corps of professionally prepared adult educators available to provide leadership for our field. But for their expertise to be utilized, employers must acquire an appreciation of their potential.

Teachers in adult education programs are typically part-time, lack employment security, and are paid a lower wage than are teachers who are hired to handle the "regular" students in colleges, extension departments, and public schools. Those who oppose the professionalization of the teacher force fail to realize that they are abetting those who would exploit these underpaid part-time teachers with no security of employment and hence no full-time career.

Emergence of Professional Associations

I have observed that where two or three educators of adults are gathered together, one of them is likely to suggest that they form an organization. If they do, it is probably because they believe that no existing adult education organization is giving adequate attention to their own favorite area of the field. The organizations that they form to serve narrow segments of the field seldom achieve political clout. They are most likely to find their efforts at securing public funding thwarted by champions of other special interest groups. Professional associations established by those who conceive of the field from a limited perspective do nothing to increase the number of overall learning opportunities or to improve the quality of existing opportunities.

National Adult Education Associations

Franklin Spikes, current president of AAACE, has said that "it is now time for members of the adult and continuing education community (in the largest sense) to set aside the boundaries established as a result of disciplinary provincialism. . . . We must move from the parochial view of our splinter groups to positions that look at what is most beneficial for the profession at large" (Spikes, 1989, pp. 68–69). What is needed is a national organizational structure that can effectively bring the diverse groups together into one association that can represent the common and combined interests of the entire field. This change can come about only through the leadership of adult educators who understand the field.

Brockett (1989, p. 117) identified the challenge as that of balancing unification and specialization, noting that without an awareness of the need for unification, "the field will inevitably continue to suffer from fragmentation and lack of professional identity." This challenge of arriving at the optimal balance of unification and specialization concerns has stymied the leadership of the American Association of Adult Educators (AAAE), AEA/USA, and AAACE and may account for the inability of any of these three associations to achieve recognition and acceptance as *the* umbrella organization for the field. The net result is that adult educators collectively are invisible politically.

A Growing Cadre of Emerging Leaders

Throughout our field, the emerging leadership is composed of individuals who have gone through rigorous programs of graduate study. Universities, state and federal education departments, and even business and industry now find it possible and desirable to employ doctoral graduates of adult education programs. A cadre of well-prepared graduates is available, and they are surely as competent as those who hold degrees in other areas. To suggest that those who are currently in the adult education field must go outside for its leaders is indeed a derogatory comment on the quality of those who have chosen this career field. Self-anointed messiahs may command a following by clever emotional appeals to the naive. Serious ethical leaders eschew the cultivation of popular prejudices and the use of false claims and promises to attract disciples to a narrow sector of the field.

Perspective Deformation of Imported Leadership

Those who have been diligent in pursuing other disciplines or social causes often suffer from "perspective deformation," exhibiting a narrowness of vision, an overcommitment to a single sector of the field, or an overdependence on their disciplinary roots. Morse Cartwright, longtime executive director of AAAE, opposed those who would have adult education become synonymous with social action, not because he was opposed to social action but because he had a broader vision of the entire field than held by social advocates such as Joseph Hart, Harry Overstreet, and Eduard Lindeman (Stubblefield and Keane, 1989), each of whom wanted to redefine the field to serve his own objectives. By espousing a single overriding purpose for adult education, whether it is empowerment or literacy, an individual abdicates any claim to leadership for the entire field.

Building a Knowledge Base

Boyd, Apps, and Associates (1980), in discussing the knowledge base of adult education, objected to the indiscriminate borrowing of concepts from the established disciplines. They did so because they perceived that adult educators need first to see clearly the "unique and particular configurations of adult education" (1980, pp. 2-3). Although they have been falsely accused of advising adult educators to reject all concepts advanced by scholars in other fields, they have in fact argued for systematic and analytical reformulation of such concepts to ensure their applicability to our field before their adoption for adult education practice. They sought to prevent the deformation of the field that would result from wholesale indiscriminate adoption of disciplinary constructs imposed from other areas, often by experts in those areas.

Exemplary Leadership

J. Roby Kidd and Malcolm Knowles are two outstanding examples of expert practitioners who aspired to enlarge their leadership and turned to graduate study as the logical approach. In Canada, J. Roby Kidd, an individual whose skill as an agent animateur was internationally recognized and who founded the International Council for Adult Education, was the first Canadian to earn a doctorate in adult education. He pursued his doctorate (at Columbia University) because he believed that intuition and experience alone were not sufficient to serve as the foundation for exemplary leadership in adult education (Thomas, 1987). In the United States, Malcolm Knowles, an expert in group dynamics and informal adult education who had already become the first executive director of AEA/USA, recognized the limits of his previous education and practical experience and so sought his doctorate at the University of Chicago. Their perspectives embraced the entire field, not just one sector or one cause (Griffith, 1991).

Historical Perspective

Prior to 1935, no adult educators had had an opportunity to pursue a doctoral program in their chosen field. Nevertheless, insightful educators of various kinds perceived adults' educational needs and sought to satisfy those needs to the best of their abilities. Some of these individuals came from established disciplines; others came from social movements that sought to use adult education as an instrument to advance their favorite causes. But since that time over four thousand women and men have earned their doctorates in adult education and are working in every conceivable setting, planning educational programs to facilitate the improvement of the quality of life of all. If we in the field look outside for our leaders, we shall surely find that the field will be redefined and shaped by their perceptions of appropriate clientele, content, method, staffing, and financing. Necessity left no choice historically, for there were no academically prepared persons prepared to bear the burdens of serving as leaders. *But the situation has changed!*

Yesterday's Solutions Fit Yesterday's Problems. If we do not reflect on the conditions that existed in the first half of this century, we might well delude ourselves into believing that nothing has changed and so the process of identifying leaders for our field ought to remain forever in the historical pattern. But if we consider that yesterday's conditions led to yesterday's practices, and if we acknowledge that significant changes have occurred in our society, then we ought logically examine the extent to which yesterday's approach to the selection of leadership is appropriate for the twenty-first century.

Today's Problems Require Contemporary Solutions. Romantic interpretations of our traditions and the history of adult education in North America lead impressionable individuals to believe that since the field was pioneered by those who acted out of instinct and personal commitment without benefit of advanced study of their field, this approach is still appropriate. But the world does not stand still; changes are all around us. Piecemeal approaches that focus on only a single aspect of the field to the exclusion of all of the rest are no longer appropriate. We cannot afford to yield to the siren song of those whose grasp of the field is limited to a single sector and whose vision is restricted to only a fragment. If we are to progress toward providing improved and enlarged learning opportunities for all, we must have leaders from within adult education who have breadth of vision and a commitment to cultivating and encouraging emerging leadership from within so as to increase the political visibility and potency of the field and thereby expand and improve educational opportunities for all.

References

Boyd, R. D., Apps, J. W., and Associates. *Redefining the Discipline of Adult Education.* San Francisco: Jossey-Bass, 1980.

Brockett, R. G. "Professional Associations for Adult and Continuing Education." In S. B. Merriam and P. M. Cunningham (eds.), *Handbook of Adult and Continuing Education.* San Francisco: Jossey-Bass, 1989.

Griffith, W. S. "Has Adult and Continuing Education Fulfilled Its Early Promise?" In B. A. Quigley (ed.), *Fulfilling the Promise of Adult and Continuing Education.* New Directions for Continuing Education, no. 44. San Francisco: Jossey-Bass, 1989.

Griffith, W. S. "The Impact of Intellectual Leadership." In J. M. Peters and P. Jarvis (eds.), *Adult Education: Evolution and Achievements in a Developing Field of Study.* San Francisco: Jossey-Bass, 1991.

Houle, C. O. "The Emergence of Graduate Study in Adult Education." In G. Jensen, A. A. Liveright, and W. Hallenbeck (eds.), *Adult Education: Outlines of an Emerging Field of University Study.* Washington, D.C.: Adult Education Association of the U.S.A., 1964.

Koloski, J. A. "Enhancing the Field's Image Through Professionalism and Practice." In B. A. Quigley (ed.), *Fulfilling the Promise of Adult and Continuing Education.* New Directions for Continuing Education, no. 44. San Francisco: Jossey-Bass, 1989.

National University Continuing Education Association. *CHEL "Next Generation" Survey.* Washington, D.C.: National University Continuing Education Association, 1989.

Spikes, W. F. "Developing Our Own Professional Associations and Building Bridges to Others." In B. A. Quigley (ed.), *Fulfilling the Promise of Adult and Continuing Education.* New Directions for Continuing Education, no. 44. San Francisco: Jossey-Bass, 1989.

Stubblefield, H. W., and Keane, P. "The History of Adult and Continuing Education." In S. B. Merriam and P. M. Cunningham (eds.), *Handbook of Adult and Continuing Education.* San Francisco: Jossey-Bass, 1989.

Thomas, A. M. "Roby Kidd—Intellectual Voyageur." In P. Jarvis (ed.), *Twentieth-Century Thinkers in Adult Education.* New York: Croom-Helm and Methuen, 1987.

WILLIAM S. GRIFFITH *is professor of adult education at the University of British Columbia, Vancouver, and past president of the American Association for Adult and Continuing Education.*

PART FOUR

Should Adult and Continuing Education Be Market Driven?

Adult and continuing education should not be market driven because market-driven systems perpetuate social inequality, they are inefficient at meeting social needs, and profit often replaces education as the primary goal.

Adult and Continuing Education Should Not Be Market Driven

Hal Beder

As I have argued before (Beder, 1981), adult and continuing education should not be market driven. I have arrived at this position through experience and scholarship, and my opinions have changed little over the years. In this chapter, my argument is based on three basic points. First, market-driven delivery systems are inherently unequal; they maximize benefits to the educationally, socially, and economically advantaged while they minimize benefits to the disadvantaged. Second, while market-driven delivery systems can be relatively efficient mechanisms for meeting individual needs and preferences, they are not efficient for meeting critical societal needs. Third, market-driven delivery systems often promote goal displacement to the extent that profit maximization replaces educational benefit as the overriding goal for adult and continuing education.

Before I address these points in depth, it is first important to clarify what a market is and then to define the term *market driven*. According to Kotler (1975, p. 23), "A market is a distinct group of people and/or organizations that have resources which they want to exchange, or might conceivably exchange, for distinct benefits." As Kotler's definition implies, market-driven systems are governed by reciprocal voluntary exchange between participants and programs. In participating, voluntary learners give up valued resources, such as time and money, to acquire something that they value more: education or training. In offering adult and continuing education, programs provide what learners value and utilize the resources that learners relinquish to operate and maintain the program. Learners' time represents enrolled clients, a basic necessity for all adult and continuing education programs. Learners' money, in the form of fees, finances market-driven programs. If sufficient numbers of learners are unwilling or unable to effect the change of resources, programs cannot survive in the marketplace and they go out of business.

The concept of exchange, the critical element of market-driven systems, is related to the concept of demand, which can be defined as the extent to which voluntary learners are willing to participate in program offerings. When motivation is high, demand is positive. When there is no motivation to participate among potential learners, there is no demand; and when learners actually choose to avoid program offerings, demand is negative. Demand is not the same as need. Frequently, adults "need" learning that they are not willing to acquire. For example, although low-literate adults may need adult literacy education, less than 8 percent of those who are eligible for instruction participate (Pugsley, 1990).

For a market-driven system to succeed, then, there must be sufficient numbers of voluntary adult learners who are motivated to exchange enough of their time and money to yield the clients and fee income that adult and continuing education programs require to operate. For this reason, market-driven systems must necessarily target their offerings on areas of high demand.

Before I move from a general discussion of market-driven systems, it is necessary to clarify the distinction between market-affected systems and market-driven systems. In a capitalistic political economy, virtually all providers of adult and continuing education are affected by market economies. Taxpayers, for example, are willing to subsidize the Cooperative Extension Service because they believe that they will benefit from higher-quality and less expensive agricultural products, and industries subsidize employee training and development in order to compete more effectively in their markets. Market-affected systems differ from market-driven systems in one critical respect, however. In market-driven systems, the resources that learners exchange to participate are the sole or primary source of operating resources for programs. Programs are thus dependent on voluntary participation and learners' fee income for their survival, and the market determines *what* is offered and *to whom*.

Market-Driven Systems Perpetuate Inequality

As Levin (1989) notes, according to human capital theory and a wealth of corroborating research, investments in education result in increased productivity and a corresponding increase in income and socioeconomic status for those who invest. If those who participate in adult and continuing education so benefit, and if more advantaged adults are more likely to participate, then through adult education the advantaged become more advantaged, and, relatively speaking, the disadvantaged become more disadvantaged.

More advantaged adults are clearly more likely to participate in adult and continuing education, a fact that has been well documented over many years (Johnstone and Rivera, 1965; Carp, Peterson, and Roelfs, 1975; U.S. Department of Education, 1986). Adults of low socioeconomic status are the least likely to participate. As reported by Merriam and Caffarella (1991, p. 67), in 1984 the participation rate in adult and continuing education was 88 percent for whites and 6 percent for blacks. For those with four years of high school, the participation rate was 30 percent; and for those with eight or less years of schooling the comparable figure was 2 percent. For adults with incomes under $12,500, the participation rate was 3 percent; and for those whose incomes were between $25,000 and $39,999, the participation rate was 11 percent. Whites are more likely than blacks to receive employer-based education, even when age and educational level are controlled (Zemsky, Tierney, Berg, and Scach-Marquez, 1983).

Why are more advantaged adults more likely to participate in adult education? Mincer (1989, p. 28) provides an answer: "Persons who have greater learning ability and better opportunities to finance the costs of human capital investments do invest more in all forms of human capital, including schooling and job training." Thus, following Mincer, there are at least two reasons why advantaged adults are more likely to participate in market-driven adult education: They have more resources to exchange for adult education offerings, and they possess more advanced learning skills.

Poor people, those who might benefit the most from participation, can less afford to pay fees. Nor can they afford the hidden costs of participation such as transportation and child care. While employers often subsidize the costs of participating in continuing education for employees, these subsidies are not available to the unemployed.

Although the disadvantaged certainly have the capacity to learn, their participation in formal adult education is often constrained by lack of prerequisite learning skills. Quite simply, the more one knows, the more options one has for continued learning. Low-literate adults are unlikely to enroll in courses that require substantial reading or mathematical ability. Adults whose previous experience with schooling was negative are unlikely to engage in similar activities.

Clearly, if the delivery system for adult and continuing education is to foster equality, it must provide opportunities for the educationally disadvantaged to acquire the skills needed to participate fully in continued education. However, because the disadvantaged lack the resources to exchange for market-driven adult education, market-driven systems cannot provide this opportunity.

Meeting Social Needs

The benefits obtained from participation in adult and continuing education accrue to both individuals and to society in general. Individuals benefit by increasing their incomes and by enhancing the quality of their lives. Society benefits from a more productive work force, a citizenry that is able to make intelligent democratic decisions, and the provision of social and economic opportunity. As a principle of public policy, when the benefits of participating in adult and continuing education accrue primarily to individuals, individuals should pay the cost of instruction (Beder, 1981). In such cases, a market-driven system is clearly appropriate. Conversely, when society is the primary beneficiary of adult and continuing education, public subsidy is warranted as an inducement to participation.

Market-driven systems are inefficient mechanisms for providing the social benefits that we all enjoy, and the reason has to do with the demand for adult and continuing education. When adult education programs are established to address social needs, there is nothing to guarantee that demand for these programs will be sufficiently high among targeted clients to yield participation. When demand for programs targeted at social benefit is low or negative, programs cannot survive in a market-driven system.

Adult literacy education provides a case in point. In analyzing the demand for adult literacy education, I divided the target population into three groups (Beder, 1991). The first was defined as the demand population. For this group, demand for adult literacy education is high enough that learners are willing to overcome the constraints to participation. This is the group that participates in adult literacy education. It is a relatively small group. The federal adult literacy program currently serves about 7 percent of those eligible per year, and the participation rate in adult basic education (excluding English as a Second Language programs) has actually declined in the past ten years (Pugsley, 1990). While some of the demand population might be willing to participate in a market-driven system, clearly their numbers are very small.

The second group was defined by those whose participation in adult literacy education is constrained, even though demand is positive. Typical constraints include lack of child care and transportation and presence of scheduling conflicts. Clearly, if the constrained are to participate, the constraining factors must be reduced or eliminated. This goal can only be achieved through provision of support services and increased program availability. Both strategies are expensive, however, and in all likelihood would raise the cost of instruction to a level that could not be sustained in a market-driven system.

The third group was defined by those for whom there is either no demand or negative demand for adult literacy education. We do not know how large this group is, but they probably are a majority. This group lacks demand because they do not perceive a need for adult literacy education and/or because their previous experiences with schooling were negative. This group will not participate voluntarily in adult literacy education, despite the social benefits, unless there are substantial inducements. These inducements, which might include substantial investment in new delivery systems and program models as well as direct stipends to learners, could never be offered without substantial public subsidy. Clearly, a market-driven system would be ill-advised as a means of serving this group.

Goal Displacement

An examination of the professional literature of adult and continuing education from the 1920s to the present leads to the conclusion that the overriding purpose of adult and continuing education is to meet individual and societal needs (Beder, 1989). Achievement of this purpose is not impossible in market-driven systems. Indeed, there are those who would argue that by targeting offerings on learners' demand, market-driven systems guarantee that learners will receive what they value. As Sulkin (1981, p. 170) notes, "When the learner has to pay for his education, he will look for relevance and the institution will be forced to come up with cost-effective alternate methods instead of subsidy requests for public funding."

There are problems with this logic, however. Although adult and continuing educators may wish to maximize educational goals, continuing education agencies are typically attached to parent institutions that view continuing education as a function supporting the goals of the larger institution. All too often parent institutions support continuing education because of the money that it earns. Thus, in market-driven systems, programmers must often meet two expectations: learners' expectations for relevant programs and their parent institutions' expectations for profit.

The need to maximize profits forces many continuing education programs to target programs on areas of high demand and on clients who have ample resources to exchange. Needy learners who do not have resources to exchange are not served. Needed programs for which there are small numbers of potential clients are not offered. Indeed, when the profit expectations of parent institutions are high, and when the success of continuing education is evaluated according to the income generated, profit maximization replaces satisfaction of educational need as the primary goal of adult and continuing education. Adult and continuing education is thus transformed into a market-driven business in which market forces determine who will be served and what programs will be offered and learning need becomes of secondary importance.

Implications for Policy and Practice

The arguments developed here suggest the following implications for policy. First, the delivery system for adult and continuing education should be organized around the principle of who benefits. When the benefits of adult and continuing education accrue primarily to individuals, and when those individuals have the means to pay for continued education, they should pay the cost of instruction. In such cases, a market-driven system is warranted. Similarly, when organizations are the primary beneficiaries of continuing education, they should subsidize adult and continuing education. However, when society at large benefits from adult and continuing education more than does the individual, adult and continuing education should receive public subsidy and should not be market driven.

Second, since market-driven systems are inherently unequal, the issue of social equality must be addressed by providing public subsidy to programs targeted to the disadvantaged. This subsidy must not only induce participation but also redress deficits in learning skills that deter the disadvantaged from full participation in the adult and continuing education system.

Third, the tendency of market-driven systems to maximize profit over learning need should be addressed by the establishment of a code of ethics and the infusion of that code into the professional norms of the field. Adult and continuing educators should feel obligated to subsidize needed programs that lose money from the profits earned by lucrative programs. Fees for high-demand programs should not be inflated merely to maximize profit. The code should also address truth in advertising. Advertising designed to create demand where demand does not exist should be avoided; advertising that accurately describes what learners will learn should be promoted.

References

Beder, H. W. "Adult Education Should Not Require Self-Support from Learners' Fees." In B. W. Kreitlow and Associates, *Examining Controversies in Adult Education*. San Francisco: Jossey-Bass, 1981.

Beder, H. W. "Purposes and Philosophies of Adult Education." In S. B. Merriam and P. M. Cunningham (eds.), *Handbook of Adult and Continuing Education*. San Francisco: Jossey-Bass, 1989.

Beder, H. W. *Adult Literacy: Issues for Policy and Practice*. Malabar, Fla.: Krieger, 1991.

Carp, A., Peterson, R., and Roelfs, P. "Adult Learning Interests and Experiences." In K. P. Cross and J. Valley (eds.), *Planning Non-Traditional Programs*. San Francisco: Jossey-Bass, 1975.

Johnstone, J. W., and Rivera, R. J. *Volunteers for Learning: A Study of the Educational Pursuits of American Adults*. Hawthorne, N.Y.: Aldine, 1965.

Kotler, P. *Marketing for Nonprofit Organizations*. Englewood Cliffs, N.J.: Prentice Hall, 1975.

Levin, H. M. "Mapping the Economics of Education: An Introductory Essay." *Educational Researcher*, 1989, *18* (4), 13–16.

Merriam, S. B., and Caffarella, R. S. *Learning in Adulthood: A Comprehensive Guide*. San Francisco: Jossey-Bass, 1991.

Mincer, J. "Human Capital and the Labor Market: A Review of Current Research." *Educational Researcher*, 1989, *18* (4), 27–34.

Pugsley, R. *Vital Statistics: Who Is Served by the Adult Education Program?* Washington, D.C.: Government Printing Office, 1990.

Sulkin, H. A. "Fees Should Support Adult Education." In B. W. Kreitlow and Associates, *Examining Controversies in Adult Education*. San Francisco: Jossey-Bass, 1981.

U.S. Department of Education. Office of Educational Research and Improvement. Center for Statistics. *Bulletin*. Washington, D.C.: Government Printing Office, 1986.

Zemsky, R., Tierney, M., Berg, I., and Scach-Marquez, J. *Training's Benchmarks. A Statistical Sketch of Employer-Provided Training and Education, 1969–1981. Task 1 Report: The Impact of Public Policy on Education and Training in the Private Sector.* Washington, D.C.: National Institute of Education, 1983.

HAL BEDER is associate professor of adult education at Rutgers University, New Brunswick, New Jersey. He has served as the president of the New Jersey Association for Lifelong Learning and as editor of Adult Education Quarterly.

Administrative units in adult and continuing education have increasingly been required to be market driven. Programs in adult continuing education are often required to be self-supporting and in some cases to return residual profits to the institution or agency.

Adult and Continuing Education Should Be Market Driven

Robert C. Mason

Among institutional governing boards, output-driven statistics and market-driven ideas for funding and programming are increasingly emphasized. Marketing is viewed differently by many in education. For some, it means that the continuing education activities must pay for themselves or generate profits to other parts of the organization or agency through fee income. Few people currently identify market-driven activities with needs assessment and marketing research as well as with pricing and promotion in meeting the needs of the various target populations. The term *market-driven adult and continuing education* and the term *marketing* are used interchangeably in this chapter.

What Is My Position?

My position is that adult and continuing education must be market driven or it will probably fail in the near future, if it has not failed already. This position is based on my knowledge and definition of marketing as involving not only sales and promotion, cost recovery, and profits but also the meeting of people's needs. Market-driven adult continuing education can also mean total support with tax dollars or foundation resources and not any support from fee income paid by the participants. Moreover, it is my position that the graduate programs designed to educate people for adult and continuing education positions are not providing adequate professional preparation for marketing, budgeting, leadership, evaluation, and accountability.

Recent dramatic budget reductions for adult and continuing education and extension activities would lead one to conclude that there is a paucity of effective leadership in adult continuing education, involving a poor understanding of marketing and a lack of marketing ideas. Bennis (1984) claimed that leadership, more than any other factor, can empower others and ultimately determine which organizations fail or succeed regardless of changing strategies, processes, or cultures. Leaders who have a clear vision of the future and of the missions of their agencies can enhance market-driven ideas for the field of adult continuing education. For example, when I was developing the graduate program in adult and continuing education for Northern Illinois University and was the only full-time professor in the field, I discovered from external consultants that generally between 70 and 80 percent of the adult continuing education graduates at that time were placed in some type of administrative or coordinative position in the field of continuing education. Yet, most graduate programs in adult continuing education focus more on general issues and research than on the professional preparation of adult continuing education leaders who really understand the concepts of market-driven continuing education. Leaders of adult continuing education should have skills that enable them to relate effectively to nonprofit organizations, college presidents, school superintendents, corporate leaders, and others who are vitally important to the future of the field.

The advent of strategic planning, primarily led by Keller (1983), enhanced the development of leadership and strategic planning to a certain extent in the administrative units of continuing education, but little effort has been made to develop updated leadership and strategic planning courses in adult continuing education, which would result in market-driven continuing education. Keller's (1983) book, *Academic Strategy: The Management Revolution in Higher Education,* has been acclaimed by Marchese (1988) as a best-seller that has done more to change higher education than any other book written on the topic. Marchese claims that when the book first appeared, only one in ten institutions had given strategic planning any thought. By 1990, well over half of the higher education institutions in the United States were involved in some type of strategic planning. Those continuing educators who ignore strategic planning and market-driven ideas will likely fall behind in or be removed from the field of continuing education, and remaining continuing education activities will probably be decentralized or reallocated to a college or subunit where they may or may not be effective.

If the adult continuing education graduate program curriculum was market driven, both professors and students would probably emphasize the problem of illiteracy. Illiteracy represents an enormous national problem in the United States today. Continuing educators in institutions of higher education, whether in graduate programs or administrative units, have a responsibility to solve the problem of illiteracy. Despite the magnitude of the problem, and despite the fact that literacy initiatives are taking on a new urgency both nationally and internationally, few graduate programs and few administrative units are gearing up to address illiteracy. If these programs were market driven, they would view the problem as an area of human need (Kotler and Fox, 1985), requiring the application of marketing principles and methods in needs assessment, market research, product and course development, and distribution.

Market-driven graduate programs in adult continuing education should redesign the curriculum to prepare future adult continuing educators in the basic competencies of leadership, evaluation, strategic planning, marketing, and budgeting, as well as in understanding how adults learn and the history and philosophy of the field. All of these subject areas should be integrated to help adult continuing educators deal effectively with societal needs. If marketing is practiced as Kotler and Fox (1985), Simerly and Associates (1989), and others define it, curriculum and learning activities in adult continuing education will be designed to serve human needs based on needs assessment and market research. These are necessary practices of adult continuing education. However, most adult continuing educators maintain the stereotype of marketing as selling and promotion aimed toward recovery of the full cost of continuing education activities.

How I Arrived at This Position and Viewpoint

I have arrived at my position through thirty years of experience as an adult and continuing educator at the high school level, corporate level, community college level, and university level. My position on market-driven adult continuing education was formulated through work as a practitioner in the field, teaching adult classes at night in a high school where the courses were market driven, as the first administrator of continuing education at a major community college, as the first person hired at a university to design and lead the development of a graduate program, and as an administrator serving in a dean's office and a research office of continuing education for eleven years. My experience has been complemented by my study of marketing, primarily through Kotler and Fox (1985), Simerly and Associates (1989), and Keller (1983), and attendance at workshops where these and other people were featured presenters and consultants. Publications from the Learning Resources Network of Manhattan, Kansas, especially the work of Collins (1982), have greatly influenced me.

During my experience as an associate dean and then acting dean of continuing education, I noted that learning experiences designed primarily for the benefit of professors or for the institution tended to fail. In contrast, successful activities were based on needs assessment, market research, and participatory involvement of the stakeholders affected by the learning experience. My understanding of marketing as more than sales, promotion, and cost recovery or fee generation also has led me to promote market-driven adult continuing education.

How Has My Position Changed Over Time?

My position has evolved since my start in continuing education in 1961. My position changed at an incremental pace when I noted an emphasis in programs on continuing professional education for doctors, lawyers, teachers, engineers, and others who could afford to pay for it. This emphasis was not necessarily market driven in accordance with the definition of marketing but was simply the offering of courses to those who could afford to pay for them. Generally, the continuing education students enrolled because of state policy mandating continuing professional education activity. Overall, as I have gained more experience in higher education leadership roles, my support of market-driven adult continuing education has grown stronger.

What Literature Supports My Position?

Kotler and Fox (1985) indicate that most people identify marketing with selling and promotion. Only a few people out of three hundred educational administrators surveyed by Kotler and Fox knew that marketing involved needs assessment, marketing research, product development, and distribution. According to Kotler and Fox, marketing is a central concern of modern institutions, growing out of a quest to effectively serve areas of human need. Simerly and Associates (1989) and Kotler and Fox (1985) claim that imposition of a program or service that is not matched to market needs or wants will fail because effective marketing is client centered, not seller centered.

Aslanian (1988) supports this view. She surveyed institutions and adults throughout the nation and found that groups of adult learners prefer cohort groups, weekend meetings, and the concentration of large blocks of time for adults to take classes. If given what they want or if the learning activities are market driven, these adults will register for adult learning experiences in large numbers. For example, Columbia University Teachers College has large enrollments in the weekend program for doctoral students. Northern Illinois University now features several cohort groups on both the master's and the doctoral levels. Smith (1991) noted that cohort group programs have moved away from traditionalism, especially the Ed.D. programs that are modeled closely after traditional Ph.D. programs, and have been developed more into what might be called the law school model: a largely preset curriculum of about three years' duration with groups of students admitted and moving through together as a class, a schedule built to accommodate continued employment with accelerated part-time study, an emphasis on leadership and policy studies skills with traditional specializations added after graduation by those students who need them, and a mechanism to encourage dissertation completion in one or two years.

This type of cohort program is market driven because most of the people who enroll are not full-time students and need a program that permits them to continue their full-time jobs. Based on my personal experience, the intellectual capabilities of the students enrolled in cohort programs equal or exceed the capabilities of those enrolled in traditional programs.

An additional benefit of the market-driven approach is that learning experiences are designed at times and places convenient to adult learners. Often, adult learners are willing to pay premium fees for market-driven learning experiences; in fact, they are willing to pay the full cost of the program in most cases. Generally, students pay somewhere between 20 and 30 percent of the actual total cost of a program offered at public universities, but the cohort groups pay the full cost or three to four times the amount that regular, traditional students pay. Market-driven adult continuing education, or, in other words, programs designed to meet the needs of learners who typically work full time, leads to satisfied learners who are willing to pay the full cost of the program. In my conversations with students, I have found that they are pleased to know in advance when courses are going to be offered, who will teach them, and what time of the month for three straight years they will be involved in coursework. This advance planning saves them hours of time driving to campus to register, hassling with the bursar or the graduate school, or dealing with closed classes. Program staff (usually continuing education coordinators) can do the coordinating work while the enrollees focus on studying. Similarly, professors can plan far ahead of time so that they know when they will be involved with the cohort group. Sometimes, a program can become market driven to the extent that it will cause the traditional daytime program to suffer; this has been the case at some institutions that have probably been more concerned about making money from these cohort groups than they have about serving people.

How Will My Position Improve Practice?

Market-driven activities can help us be more nontraditional in approach and meet the needs of our client groups both within our service regions and throughout the nation and the world through distance education activities and computer technology. Aslanian's (1988) research shows that students want learning experiences at times and places convenient to them. This convenience may involve self-directed learning packets, or it may involve distance education activities that enable them to study in their own homes or at their places of work. The new majority of adult learners is insisting on these kinds of services as opposed to the traditional services offered to eighteen- to twenty-one-year-olds. By offering continuing education programs that are truly market driven, we know that we are meeting the needs of these adult students through educational opportunities presented in the manner that they want and at times and places convenient to their work and family situations.

More market-driven activities are needed in the curricula of graduate programs of adult continuing education, and these activities should reflect the interests of students who want to learn more about market-driven continuing education. Moreover, our graduate programs of adult and continuing education need to give greater attention to where students are placed upon graduation. Between 70 and 80 percent actually go into leadership positions or are expected to develop market-driven activities or to recover the cost of these activities. They need to be prepared adequately in leadership, strategic planning, budgeting, and marketing.

Conclusion

A major problem is that most of the administrative units of adult and continuing education located within public universities, private colleges and universities, nonprofit organizations, and for-profit organizations tend to be oriented toward market-driven educational activities, whereas many of the training programs and professional preparation graduate programs in adult and continuing education do not emphasize budgeting, marketing, strategic planning, and other concepts that need to be stressed to help professionals prepare to meet the changing times which require market-driven adult continuing education programs. Dissonance between these administrative units and graduate programs will continue until the professional programs prepare personnel to effectively practice market-driven adult and continuing education.

References

Aslanian, C. B. *How Americans in Transition Study for College Credit.* New York: College Entrance Examination Board, 1988.

Bennis, W. "The 4 Competencies of Leadership." *Training and Development Journal,* Aug. 1984, pp. 20-24.

Collins, K. S. *Marketing Noncredit Courses to Business and Industry.* Manhattan, Kans.: Learning Resources Network, 1982.

Keller, G. *Academic Strategy: The Management Revolution in Higher Education.* Baltimore, Md.: Johns Hopkins University Press, 1983.

Kotler, P., and Fox, K.F.A. *Strategic Marketing for Educational Institutions.* Englewood Cliffs, N.J.: Prentice Hall, 1985.

Marchese, T. "Academic Strategy: Five Years Later." *American Association for Higher Education Bulletin,* 1988, *40* (6), 3-6.

Simerly, R. G., and Associates. *Handbook of Marketing for Continuing Education.* San Francisco: Jossey-Bass, 1989.

Smith, L. G. "Alpha and Omega: An Excursion Through Interesting Ideas . . . Pursue Them Through a Lifetime!" *Leadership and Educational Policy Studies Newsletter,* 1991, *5* (1), 2-7.

ROBERT C. MASON is professor of adult and continuing education and director of the Office of Research in Adult Continuing Education at Northern Illinois University, De Kalb.

PART FIVE

Should Continuing Education
Be Mandatory?

The negative consequences of mandatory continuing education outweigh potential benefits.

Do We Really Need Mandatory Continuing Education?

Ralph G. Brockett

Mandatory continuing education (MCE) is a very seductive idea. It can be used as a basis for society to assume that professionals (and sometimes individuals in nonprofessional roles) have met minimum participation requirements. In this way, MCE is sometimes believed to serve as a "consumer protection" mechanism against professionals who are unwilling or unable to keep up with current developments in their field. It is also used as a means of "rehabilitation" for individuals who have failed to function as productive members of our society (for instance, prison inmates seeking parole, persons convicted of driving under the influence of alcohol, or individuals receiving public assistance payments). Still another apparent benefit of MCE is that it can help facilitate the growth of the adult and continuing education field by securing a central place for the education of adults within society and by providing more career opportunities for educators of adults.

My personal interest in the MCE issue dates back more than a decade. Upon considerable reflection and with the benefit of many discussions with students and colleagues over several years, I continue to support the position that I have held for many years: The potential negative consequences of MCE far outweigh benefits that might be gained from such activities. My position is based on three main points: (1) MCE violates central principles of adult education practice, (2) MCE creates a "punitive" attitude toward participation in adult and continuing education, and (3) MCE does not ensure effective or competent performance. In this chapter, I elaborate on these three points and offer an alternative way of thinking about the issue. But, first, I share some thoughts on how my position has developed and evolved over time.

NEW DIRECTIONS FOR ADULT AND CONTINUING EDUCATION, no. 54, Summer 1992 © Jossey-Bass Publishers

Reflections on an Evolving Position

I first became interested in the MCE issue during the 1979 National Adult Education Conference in Boston, shortly after entering a doctoral program in adult education. At that conference, I first met John Ohliger, who was one of the most outspoken critics of MCE. Over dinner one evening, he shared his position with me and told me of the National Alliance for Voluntary Learning (NAVL), an informal group that was sponsoring several meetings during the conference. I attended some of these sessions and had the opportunity to meet others who opposed MCE. NAVL was very visible during this conference and helped to create an atmosphere that was simultaneously thought-provoking and fun. By the end of the conference, I felt a kinship with the group and many of its members.

During the next year, the MCE issue received increasing attention. The former Adult Education Association of the U.S.A. (now the American Association for Adult and Continuing Education) appointed the Task Force on Voluntary Learning to meet and discuss the issue. The work of this group resulted in the publication of a report containing several position statements (Heaney, 1980). In addition, Basic Choices, Inc., published *Second Thoughts,* a newsletter devoted to raising questions about MCE and similar concerns. Both the task force's report and *Second Thoughts* were filled with powerful and passionate perspectives on the hazards of MCE. For instance, Day (1980, p. 5) offered the following position: "Compulsory adult education is a repulsive idea. It always has been. Forcing individuals to further their education— undisguised in the case of mandatory continuing professional education, somewhat concealed in promotion considerations which require advanced degrees or certification—is antithetical to the ideals which the early American adult education movement cherished." One issue of *Second Thoughts* included statements by several professors of adult education. The following are some of the points that were particularly important to me at the time: "We have sufficient knowledge of educational design and educational promotion to attract people to our programs. We don't need captive audiences, do we?" (Smith, 1980, p. 3). "If adult educators jump on the MCE bandwagon, the field may flourish for a while—until the public discovers that the emperors of adult education have as few clothes as the emperors of schooling" (Carlson, 1980, p. 3). "Forced participation in continuing education seems to me seldom if ever justifiable. If the issue is maintenance of competency to practice some occupation, then competency should be enforced, not sitting in classrooms" (Darkenwald, 1980, p. 4). "What bothers me most about the acceleration of MCE is the frequent ignorance about or denial of the propensity of most adults toward self-guided study . . . what prompts the MCE advocate to suggest that professional competence must be maintained primarily through attendance in structured, institutionally sponsored continuing education offerings?" (Hiemstra, 1980, p. 5).

As I reflect on my early exposure to the MCE controversy, what remains most clearly in my mind is the emotion-charged climate and enthusiasm with which critics tackled the issue. For me, it was a most exciting way to become involved with the field, and I am concerned that this kind of spirit is largely lacking in our associations and professional literature today.

In the years since I first became interested in MCE, I have had many opportunities to discuss the issue informally with colleagues in the field and in many of the graduate classes that I have taught. As a result, over the years I have heard some thoughtful arguments that have led me to temper my own position. For instance, a former professor of mine once asked whether it is even appropriate for adult educators to be involved in the MCE debate, or whether this is a matter to be decided by members of the professions affected. On another occasion, a graduate student pointed out that in some cases MCE might be the only way for professionals to "justify" taking the time and to receive employer support for participation in continuing education activities. Thus, while I have retained the basic tenets that framed my early thinking about MCE, I am now better able to understand and appreciate—although continuing to disagree with—reasons for supporting MCE.

Three Reasons to Oppose MCE

As I stated at the outset of this chapter, my opposition to MCE rests largely on three major points. Let us look briefly at each of these.

MCE Violates Basic Principles of Adult Education. Voluntary participation has been one of adult education's most enduring qualities. Lindeman ([1926] 1989) and Bryson (1936), in the first textbook on U.S. adult education, were very clear on this point. One of the hallmarks distinguishing adult education from other sectors of the education enterprise has been the idea that "adults vote with their feet": If adults do not perceive benefits to what they are learning, they likely choose not to continue the program. One would be hard-pressed to think of a better way to ensure quality educational programming. Yet, the mandating of these activities can negate this powerful principle.

Another principle that risks violation through MCE is the informal nature of adult education. While some MCE requirements allow and even encourage a degree of informal learning activity (see, for example, Campbell, 1982), the potential harm of MCE comes in the form of creating increasingly more formal programs while, in order to increase enrollments, encouraging learners to question the value of what they learn informally in self-directed or small group settings.

MCE Creates a Punitive Attitude Toward Participation in Adult and Continuing Education. If one works from the assumption that most professionals, whether because they are overworked or simply lazy, do not engage in even a minimal level of continuing professional development activities, then it makes sense to mandate these activities. On the other hand, if professionals, as a whole, do engage in continuing professional development, then MCE becomes a punitive endeavor because it seeks to place sanctions on activities that are already taking place. To be sure, all professions have some individuals who are not going to keep up with their respective fields. The problem is that in order to try and "catch" such individuals, MCE requirements in effect punish the majority of professionals in order to address a problem caused by a clear minority. Why should someone who is already engaged in a systematic, successful professional development plan be required to adhere to attendance requirements simply because some of his or her colleagues are unable or unwilling to do the same?

Outside of the context of professions, the punitive nature of MCE requirements becomes even more apparent. When a safe driving course is required as part of a conviction for driving while intoxicated, it is clearly part of one's punishment. Similarly, when receipt of public assistance is tied to one's participation in an adult basic education program, a plan with good intentions quickly can become a way to manipulate individuals who already are likely to feel disenfranchised.

When adult and continuing education is used in ways such as those described above, it is defying the basic principles on which most educators agree good practice is based. In most cases, the result of requiring someone to participate will be an angry, resentful, unmotivated individual. While some educators may relish the challenge of "winning over" such learners, I would much prefer to spend my time and energy working with individuals who have made the choice to attend in the first place.

MCE Does Not Ensure Effective Performance. When we speak of MCE, a crucial point becomes clear: We can mandate participation, but we cannot make an individual learn. Once this point is clear, the case for MCE breaks down completely. Some might respond by saying that "at least if we get them to attend, some of the learning will rub off." But this is really a lame rationale. Are we willing to settle for letting a few things "rub off," or do we wish to strive for excellence in our continuing education efforts?

To date, research on MCE has been limited. However, the available research evidence provides a mixed picture. Phillips (1987, p. 59) pointed out that while some studies of physicians have been unable to demonstrate the effectiveness of continuing education programs, others have demonstrated a positive impact on the "performance of physicians or patient outcomes as a result of particular programs." Phillips argues on behalf of MCE by noting that (1) most licensees in states with MCE requirements approve of such regulations, (2) a large number of professional "laggards" are finding renewed interest in their professions and in professional activities because of involvement in MCE activities, (3) MCE requirements lead to an increased number of participants in available programs, and (4) MCE helps professions to examine new ways of improving performance. Additional evidence on behalf of MCE is offered in a research review by Hutton (1987), who concluded that while the relationship between participation in continuing education and improvement in clinical practice was inconclusive, "the evidence gleaned from the attitude and perceived impact research consistently conclude that the majority of nurses in mandatory states favor compulsory participation, and perceive more benefits than problems" with MCE (p. 212). A more recent research review by Thurston (1992) arrived at essentially the same conclusion.

On the other hand, a survey of physicians in Michigan, conducted ten years after the implementation of MCE requirements, reported that the "continuing education habits and preferences" of physicians were similar to those found in surveys prior to the implementation of MCE legislation (Stross and Harlan, 1987, p. 25). Further, the researchers failed to find improvements in patient care, reduction in the number of malpractice suits, or reduced costs of health care. In another study, DeHaven (1990) examined compliance with an employer-mandated continuing nursing education program in one hospital. In finding that a high percentage of the nurses exceeded requirements, DeHaven concluded that the MCE requirement was actually unnecessary. Finally, Frye (1990) conducted a comparative analysis of MCE in law and medicine. She concluded that although MCE requirements have not detracted from the quality of continuing education programs for these professionals and may, in fact, actually lead to improved quality of and access to these programs, MCE does not guarantee professional competence because "the overall impact of continuing education cannot be proven conclusively" (1990, p. 24).

This chapter is not intended to be a comprehensive review of research. However, it is important to stress that until more evidence, based on studies employing a wide range of methodologies, becomes available, and until these studies come from a broad spectrum of professions, it is premature to argue that MCE has a positive impact on professional performance.

Mandate Performance, Not Participation

By arguing against MCE I am in no way in favor of allowing professionals to engage in outdated practices. To be sure, I am in favor of finding ways to improve professional performance and to remove individuals from practice who are unwilling or uninterested in engaging in professional growth activities. However, instead of expending time and resources on the establishment of MCE participation requirements, we should be directing our efforts toward mandating effective performance. Adult and continuing education is most often a means to some other ends. Therefore, why not shift the emphasis of a mandate from the means to the ends? For example, a professional's performance could be checked periodically in the presence of a fully credentialed colleague. This approach would be particularly warranted in cases, such as surgeons or airline pilots, where the professionals deal with life-and-death situations, because a qualified person is always available to intervene if necessary.

In conclusion, there are many different paths that can be taken to reach the goal of effective performance. By establishing MCE requirements, a profession is basically closing off alternative paths by prescribing a uniform route to effective performance. On the other hand, voluntary participation puts responsibility on the learner and is consistent with most conceptions of "good" adult and continuing education practice. While MCE may in fact provide short-term benefits in some situations, the long-term costs to individuals and to society clearly outweigh the benefits.

References

Bryson, L. Adult Education. New York: American Book, 1936.

Campbell, M. D. "Mandatory Continuing Professional Education: Help or Hindrance to Quality Education?" In S. B. Merriam (ed.), Linking Philosophy and Practice. New Directions for Adult and Continuing Education, no. 15. San Francisco: Jossey-Bass, 1982.

Carlson, R. A. "MCE is THE Solution." Second Thoughts, 1980, 2 (3), 3.

Darkenwald, G. G. "Learning—Yes! MCE—No!" Second Thoughts, 1980, 2 (3), 4.

Day, M. "On Behalf of Voluntary Adult Education." In T. W. Heaney (ed.), Task Force Report. Chicago: Adult Education Association of the U.S.A. Task Force on Voluntary Learning, 1980.

DeHaven, M. M. "Compliance with Mandatory Continuing Education in Nursing: A Hospital-Based Study." Journal of Continuing Education in Nursing, 1990, 21 (3), 102–104.

Frye, S. J. "Mandatory Continuing Education for Professional Relicensure: A Comparative Analysis of Its Impact in Law and Medicine." Journal of Continuing Higher Education, 1990, 38 (1), 16–25.

Heaney, T. W. (ed.). Task Force Report. Chicago: Adult Education Association of the U.S.A. Task Force on Voluntary Learning, 1980.

Hiemstra, R. "MCE Denies Self-Study." Second Thoughts, 1980, 2 (3), 5.

Hutton, C. A. "Impact of Mandatory Continuing Education: A Review of Research on Nurses' Attitudes and Perceived Outcomes." Journal of Continuing Education in Nursing, 1987, 18 (6), 209–213.

Lindeman, E. C. The Meaning of Adult Education. Norman: Oklahoma Research Center for Continuing Higher and Professional Education, University of Oklahoma, 1989. (Originally published 1926.)

Phillips, L. E. "Is Mandatory Continuing Education Working?" Mobius, 1987, 7 (1), 57–64.

Smith, R. M. "Six Reasons to Think Twice." Second Thoughts, 1980, 2 (3), 3.

Stross, J. K., and Harlan, W. R. "Mandatory Continuing Medical Education Revisited." Mobius, 1987, 7 (1), 22–27.

Thurston, H. I. "Mandatory Continuing Education: What the Research Tells Us." Journal of Continuing Education in Nursing, 1992, 23 (1), 6–14.

RALPH G. BROCKETT is associate professor of adult education at the University of Tennessee, Knoxville, and is editor-in-chief of New Directions for Adult and Continuing Education.

Mandatory continuing education is a natural extension of the preprofessional preparation process.

A Change of Heart:
Continuing Professional
Education Should Be Mandatory

Barbara F. LeGrand

A deeply embedded tradition in adult and continuing education is that lifelong learning should be individualistic, and that adults should be empowered to direct their own educational efforts. The field has in the past several decades been heavily influenced by the humanistic philosophy that promotes self-actualization for adult learners (Knowles, 1970). For those persons who have been professionally trained and/or teach in graduate programs of adult and continuing education, the natural progression of logic is that for those adult learners who are professionals, mandatory continuing education (MCE) is inherently unfair, ineffectual, and may even be detrimental to the professionals' desire to learn (Heaney, 1980; Rockhill, 1981). The flavor of the powerful rhetoric against MCE is that it is meanspirited. Opponents often use words such as "compulsory," "force," and "social pressure."

As someone who has worked in continuing professional education (CPE) since the mid-1970s and has earned a doctorate in the field, I have had my professional values system shaped against this backdrop. Therefore, I am clearly sensitive to the unpopularity in my field of the stand favoring MCE. However, as a continuing *professional* educator, I cannot operate only in the values system of my own profession. I must understand and operate in the culture and values system of the professions that I serve. Included in this process is compromise with the professions with which I work as the people in those professions learn more about adults and adult learning.

All states have an MCE licensure requirement for one or more professions

(L. E. Phillips, personal communication, January 1992). Variations in those requirements exist from profession to profession and state to state. In some instances the requirements range from annual participation in a small number of hours of formal accredited programs to a substantial commitment of time in both formal and informal activities. A growing trend in some states and professions is the requirement of attendance in courses focusing on specific content areas, such as AIDS education for health professionals. However, licensure is not the only regulation that requires MCE. Professional associations sometimes mandate CPE participation as a criterion for certification and recertification of an individual professional. Lack of certification does not legally prevent an individual from practicing in his or her profession (Galbraith and Gilley, 1986). But the effect may be the same since certification is often used as a basis for employment and advancement.

The debate over whether continuing education for professionals should be mandatory is passé. Even though the pace of introducing new requirements has slowed in recent years, MCE in some form is here to stay (Kenny, 1985; Thurston, 1992). As a result, over the past two decades a whole generation of new professionals have been socialized to accept this requirement and develop a positive attitude toward CPE. For them, acceptance of MCE is a natural extension of the preprofessional preparation process.

My own profession must now move beyond an old argument—the simplistic yes-no and philosophical for-against argument—to accept the challenge of providing quality formal educational experiences while promoting the value of information education for the individual practitioner. As leaders in CPE, we need to act as educational advisers (Watts, 1987) to find practical solutions in an imperfect world. To be of service, continuing professional educators, therefore, must operate within the framework of MCE to address worthy, complex, and ambiguous questions such as the following: Under what circumstances and for which professions is MCE a reasonable requirement? What should be the standards of MCE? Which continuing education providers are best qualified to meet the standards of MCE? What educational methodologies can be utilized to improve participant learning and positively impact professional performance? And how can professions and states recognize these methods for awarding MCE credit? What organizational systems must be in place to implement MCE responsibly and ethically? What are the desired outcomes of MCE, and how can these be achieved most efficiently? How can quality CPE programs be made geographically and financially accessible to those professionals who need them?

My Experience as a Continuing Professional Educator

Since 1977, I have worked in a variety of capacities in CPE—program developer, professor, researcher, administrator, and consultant—primarily at the University of Illinois at Urbana-Champaign and currently at the University of Kentucky. I was introduced to CPE during the greatest heat of the MCE debate. I was present in 1980 at the Adult Education Association of the U.S.A. (now American Association for Adult and Continuing Education) annual meeting in Saint Louis when the Task Force on Voluntary Learning passed out a very negative report opposing MCE that helped to shape how my profession viewed the issue.

My first experiences with MCE as a continuing professional educator fulfilled these ominous predictions. In the late 1970s, the state of Illinois introduced a MCE licensure requirement for physicians. Confusion in implementation of accreditation standards and participant documentation in that precomputer era reigned. These early inconveniences negatively affected the opinions of both providers and professionals. It was not unusual to see psychiatrists attending our cardiology programs simply to pick up the hours necessary to maintain their licenses. The pieces of paper passed out at the end of the day seemed to have more significance than the carefully planned educational content.

After completing my doctoral program, I taught in a graduate program, including a course on CPE. The MCE debate is excellent material on controversies to use in final and doctoral qualifying examinations. Based on my experience, professional socialization, and the persuasive literature available on the topic at the time, I delighted in reading the papers of students who concluded that MCE was counterproductive.

I am now back in administration in continuing pharmacy education at the University of Kentucky. A typical requirement in most of the forty-six states with MCE legislation pertaining to pharmacists is that they must complete fifteen hours of American Council of Pharmaceutical Education accredited continuing education annually. In my experience in an office that offers continuing education programs throughout the United States, pharmacists generally accept MCE as a requirement to be a professional. In fact, pharmacists would likely find it peculiar that someone trained in adult and continuing education would oppose this standard.

My current experiences confirm the claims in the MCE literature that requirements have increased the quantity and quality of CPE programs available to professionals (Frye, 1990; Jahns, Urbano, and Urbana, 1985; Grotelueschen and Associates, 1990; Young and Company, 1987). Pharmacists and other professionals have many different opportunities to obtain the mandated hours requirement of CPE: conferences; local, state, regional, and national professional association meetings; home study courses; satellite programs; readings in professional journals; among others. At our programs, participants often comment that they have enough credit and do not need the documentation. Because of the mandated requirement, as a provider in the only college of pharmacy in the state, a main mission of the office in which I work is to reach all pharmacists in the state through a variety of delivery methods.

As requirements have increased in pharmacy and other professions, larger numbers of providers have contributed to improved program quality based on a systematic planning process. For example, the American Council of Pharmaceutical Education offers periodic workshops for providers to teach them how to plan and deliver quality educational programs. In medicine, professionally trained educators are now routinely welcomed and are assuming leadership in the field of continuing medical education (Harrison, 1991). In working with pharmacy faculty nationally, I have been impressed with their knowledge and concern about educational quality and delivery. Often, the faculty members to whom I extend invitations to conduct our programs are prepared to write educational goals and objectives, to provide me with schedules, and to develop pre- and postprogram self-assessment instruments. I feel that this sensitivity to the educational process is directly related to MCE and the accreditation process.

Reframing the Issues Against MCE: Examining New Evidence

As more research-based data emerge, it is becoming more evident that arguments against MCE are flawed. By reframing the issues, new perspectives come to light that support the appropriateness of MCE.

Participation and Professionals' Learning and Competence. An early argument against MCE was that there is no definitive evidence that a professional's participation in CPE leads to learning and, therefore, to increased professional competence (Rockhill, 1981). Research in this area has been historically limited by flaws in methodology and possibly invalid results (Frye, 1990). Evaluations of program outcomes rarely move beyond attitudinal instruments completed at the end of an educational event. When an assessment for knowledge gain is made, the variable of how well mastery of program content translates into the complex world of practice is difficult to measure. Performance-based measurements in the forms of practice audits and complex task analyses are costly and rarely used. Although the amount of research-based data demonstrating a linkage between participation in continuing education and professional competence is still limited, several recent studies have yielded promising results in that direction (Phillips, 1987). Three studies using different methodologies with distinct professions are described below.

Upon the enactment in 1985 and implementation in 1987 of its MCE legislation for licensed accountants engaged in public practice, the State of New York took advantage of the opportunity to study a variety of issues related to continuing education participation and professional practice (Grotelueschen and Associates, 1990). The researchers in this series of well-designed studies used a variety of methodologies to assess participation in continuing accounting education, knowledge gain, and attitudes toward MCE both prior to the time the legislation was implemented and during the first three years. The studies' findings consistently demonstrate a positive correlation between recent participation in continuing education activities and proficiency in both general and specific content knowledge.

Those who engaged in continuing education demonstrated the capacity in practice to use the knowledge acquired in recent courses. So conclusive are the data that not only is a continuation of the requirement recommended but also an increase in the minimum annual participation time to forty hours in general knowledge-based courses and twenty-four hours in content-specific courses on auditing, accounting, or taxation.

In a metanalysis of the health professions' literature on the effectiveness of continuing education participation in general, Nona, Kenny, and Johnson (1988, p. 116) found that many "recent and well-designed studies have been successful in documenting positive changes in health professionals' behavior and overall impact on patient outcomes." This metanalysis focused on studies that assess changes in attitudes, knowledge base, performance, and improvements in patient outcomes as a result of participation in continuing education. The findings were most definitive in those studies in which researchers conducted audits of actual or recorded performance in practice situations.

In a survey focusing on whether the California real estate mandatory continuing education licensure requirement should be continued, active and nonactive licensees reported different benefits of continuing education (Young and Company, 1987). A distinctive feature of this legislation is that not only is participation required but also licensees must pass a test to be awarded credit. Not only did a large majority of active licensees report improved currency of knowledge and license skills, but 61 percent opposed the elimination of the testing-evaluation requirement of individual courses. The nonactive licensees were less favorable about the benefits of the continuing education licensure requirement. The latter finding substantiates the claim that the greatest effect of MCE is on the "laggard" professionals or the 25 to 30 percent who do little more than the minimum to maintain their licenses. The requirement may influence those on the fence about their profession—and perhaps the least competent—to either disengage or stimulate a renewed interest in learning (Phillips, 1987).

While not abundant, research-based information is emerging that suggests participation in continuing education activities has a positive influence on a professional's learning, capacity to perform, and competence. But well-designed studies are costly, and licensing bodies lack resources to conduct systematic research consistently. Those of us who have chosen education as a field of study and practice have placed our faith in the educational process. We chose education because we believe it has a positive effect on the services that we provide and the clientele we serve. Through study and experience, many of us bring expertise and a connoisseurship to our programs to analyze their effects, a process that by necessity transcends the empirical studies that are impossible to implement for each program in the real world.

Within this imperfect system, continuing professional educators must reframe this argument in a positive direction by becoming involved in ways to strengthen the relationship between continuing education activities and professional competence. Methods include engaging professionals in the design of learning projects, giving professionals a clear concept of learning expectations, and using educational formats that are consistent with the desired program outcomes and specific situations. The outcomes assessment movement at all levels of education is gaining in popularity and sophistication (Loacker, 1991). Finding ways to strengthen these methodologies and implement them in everyday practice can reinforce the positive influences that are suggested in the few research-based studies.

Adults and Self-Direction. Another argument against MCE is that individuals are deprived of the personal freedom of choice as adult learners (Rockhill, 1981; Heaney, 1980). This compulsion is presumed to interfere with a professional's desire to engage in independent learning experiences. As a result, professionals' attitudes toward formal education activities, self-directed learning, and continuing education in general will be negative.

This argument is flawed, however, because professionals are *not* ordinary adult learners. By virtue of the socialization process, including many requirements and responsibilities, professionals waive a certain amount of freedom in order to pursue their work in ways consistent with the norms of the professional group (Mattran, 1981). Professionals are compelled to learn particular content and perform their roles in a specific manner as defined by the profession and society. Professional groups mandate pre-professional requirements such as training programs, clerkships, board examinations, internships, and residencies. The requirement of continuing education is a natural extension of the process by which professional groups set standards for individual members. When challenged, the legality of professional groups to mandate continuing education has been upheld in courts of law (for example, Supreme Court of Florida, Amendment to Rule Regulating the Florida Bar, No. 68,708, March 19, 1987).

Personal freedom of choice and self-direction in selecting continuing education come in varying degrees. Most MCE standards set broad criteria, usually in hours of participation within a specific time frame for completion. Professionals often have the latitude to choose the specific course content, provider, educational format, and location from an array of offerings. If course choice is not extensive, professionals can influence program development by working with local, state, and regional professional associations, employers, educational institutions, government, and private agencies. In some instances, contract, independent learning can be awarded continuing education credit.

Approaches now emerging in continuing education suggest that self-directed learning, even for professionals, may not be the most efficient, effective, or even safe method with which to begin continuing education (Farmer, Buckmaster, and LeGrand, 1992; Prestine and LeGrand, 1991). Some learning in professional fields has a low threshold for risk or error and should only be approached through interaction with a highly proficient or expert professional. Formal and accredited programs under these circumstances are highly appropriate and desirable. As continuing professional educators, we can take leadership in designing situation-specific educational experiences based on appropriate educational philosophies and approaches to meet accreditation and MCE requirements.

Negative "Forced" Participation. Opponents of MCE are concerned that professionals will have a negative attitude toward mandation of continuing education that will carry over into learning in general. In fact, there are many anecdotal and research-based reports indicating that the opposite has occurred. An increase in overall support for MCE requirements and their benefits to learning has been documented over time in several professions: nurses (Arneson, 1985), accountants (Grotelueschen and Associates, 1990), and real estate licensees (Young and Company, 1987).

The positive attitude toward MCE may be directly related to other positive benefits of continuing education. Professionals attending formal programs gain positive feedback about their practices, which creates a system of affirmation and validation. In addition, increased interaction with colleagues can have a positive impact on professionalism and commitment. This interaction is especially important for professionals who work in small practices. In a study of the grandfathering phase of home economist certification, the only commitment of the professionals was to engage in MCE. The results of the study revealed that home economists who chose to certify reported one or more positive consequences, increased interaction among professionals, and increased attendance at professional meetings. These individuals also experienced increased satisfaction in being home economists and greater self-esteem as professionals (Grogan, 1990). Continuing professional educators can build on this increased sense of professionalism and commitment to program planning.

Enhancing Continuing Professional Educators' Practice

The issues surrounding mandatory continuing education for professionals are complex and must be addressed carefully. By virtue of the fact that MCE is widespread in the professions, it is likely that a continuing professional educator will be working within the context of mandation. Our responsibility to the professions is, therefore, even more important. We, as experts in CPE, have an even greater ethical obligation now to design programs based on adult learning principles and our knowledge of the professions than we did under voluntary participation. In addition, as providers, we must continuously address the questions discussed here and communicate with licensing boards, accreditation agencies, professional associations, professional schools, and individual professionals.

References

Arneson, S. W. "Iowa Nurses' Attitudes Toward Mandatory Continuing Education." *Journal of Continuing Education in Nursing,* 1985, *16* (1), 13–18.

Farmer, J. A., Buckmaster, A. W., and LeGrand, B. F. "Cognitive Apprenticeship: Implications for Continuing Professional Education." In M. Baskett and V. Marsick (eds.), *Professionals' Ways of Knowing: Implications for Practice.* New Directions for Adult and Continuing Education, no. 53. San Francisco: Jossey-Bass, 1992.

Frye, S. J. "Mandatory Continuing Education for Professional Relicensure: A Comparative Analysis of Its Impact in Law and Medicine." *Journal of Continuing Higher Education,* 1990, *38* (1), 16–25.

Galbraith, M. W., and Gilley, J. W. *Professional Certification: Implications for Adult Education and HRD.* Columbus, Ohio: ERIC Clearinghouse on Adult, Career, and Vocational Education, 1986.

Grogan, S. "Grandfathering into Professional Certification from the Perspective of Members of the American Home Economics Association." Unpublished doctoral dissertation, Department of Administration, Higher and Continuing Education, University of Illinois, 1990.

Grotelueschen, A., and Associates. *An Analysis of the Effectiveness of Mandatory Continuing Education for Licensed Accountants in Public Practice in New York State.* Albany: State Board for Public Accountancy, New York State Education Department, 1990.

Harrison, R. V. "The Shift of CME Leadership from Physicians to Non-Physicians." *Journal of Continuing Education in the Health Professions,* 1991, *11,* 183–186.

Heaney, T. W. (ed.). *Task Force Report.* Chicago: Adult Education Association of the U.S.A., Task Force on Voluntary Learning, 1980.

Jahns, I., Urbano, M., and Urbana, R. "How Mandatory Is Mandatory Continuing Education?" In M. Rivera (ed.), *Proceedings of the Lifelong Learning Research Conference.* College Park: University of Maryland Press, 1985.

Kenny, W. R. "Program Planning and Accreditation." In R. M. Cervero and C. L. Scanlan (eds.), *Problems and Prospects in Continuing Professional Education.* New Directions for Adult and Continuing Education, no. 27. San Francisco: Jossey-Bass, 1985.

Knowles, M. *The Modern Practice of Adult Education.* Chicago: Follett, 1970.

Loacker, G. "Transforming the Odyssey: Curriculum as an Outcome-Directed Pathway." *American Journal of Pharmaceutical Education,* 1991, *55* (4), 360–364.

Mattran, K. J. "Mandatory Education Increases Professional Competence." In B. W. Kreitlow and Associates, *Examining Controversies in Adult Education.* San Francisco: Jossey-Bass, 1981.

Nona, D. A., Kenny, W. R., and Johnson, D. K. "The Effectiveness of Continuing Education as Reflected in the Literature of the Health Professions." *American Journal of Pharmaceutical Education,* 1988, *52* (2), 111–116.

Phillips, L. E. "Is Mandatory Continuing Education Working?" *Mobius,* 1987, *7* (1), 57–64.

Prestine, N. A., and LeGrand, B. F. "Cognitive Learning Theory and the Preparation of Educational Administrators: Implications for Practice and Policy." *Educational Administration Quarterly,* 1991, *27* (1), 6–14.

Rockhill, K. "Professional Education Should Not Be Mandatory." In B. W. Kreitlow and Associates, *Examining Controversies in Adult Education.* San Francisco: Jossey-Bass, 1981.

Thurston, H. I. "Mandatory Continuing Education: What the Research Tells Us." *Journal of Continuing Education in Nursing,* 1992, *23* (1), 6–14.

Watts, M.S.M. "Educational Advisor to Health Professionals." *Journal of Continuing Health Professions Education*, 1987, 7 (1), 46–48.

Young, A., and Company. *Review of California's Continuing Education Program.* Sacramento: California Department of Real Estate, 1987.

BARBARA F. LEGRAND is associate director of continuing pharmacy education at the University of Kentucky, Lexington.

PART SIX

Should Adult and Continuing
Education Develop a Code
of Ethics?

Institution and ideological apparatus are developed by society to keep everything in place—they are there for social control. To ensure that things do not change, we develop codes implicitly or explicitly to control behavior so that the present structure is affirmed. We can develop ethical principles involving our craft at a technical level but lose sight of a more basic and comprehensive ethic.

Adult and Continuing Education Does Not Need a Code of Ethics

Phyllis M. Cunningham

The term *code of ethics,* like apple pie and parenthood, elicits positive feelings. How could anyone be against a code of ethics? Especially an educator to whom the responsibility is given of providing an environment for the development of the mind. So my first point here is that I am for ethical behavior; my second point is that I am against formulating a code of ethics for adult continuing educators. My position supports that of Carlson (1988) and opposes that of Connelly and Light (1991), who favor the formulation of a code of ethics, arguing that the professionalization of the field depends on such a code.

My Position

I hold the position that neither the field nor an association within the field should develop a code of ethics. I see a codification of "oughts" to regulate behavior as both inappropriate and ineffective. It is inappropriate because codes are developed to privilege a group of persons who either are in or working toward gaining positions of power. Further, written codes are an ineffective means of preventing unfair, unequal, incompetent, or negligent treatment of others. A more appropriate vision is one in which all persons develop a critical reflective stance whereby the oughts for oneself or for a collective are continually and democratically negotiated. Ethics implies social behavior, so the larger question concerns how one should behave responsibly toward oneself, others, and the environment. Codes of ethics freeze the oughts in time and space, tend to decontextualize normative behavior, privilege those in power positions, and inhibit the ability of individuals or groups to reconstruct social reality.

Development of My View

My present view has emerged in a dialectical fashion from a strong base of values first experienced in my family, who celebrated personal virtue over acquisition of power or possessions. One's day-to-day behavior was expected to be an acting out of beliefs. Although at the age of nineteen I took the Florence Nightingale pledge (complete with candles in a gothic cathedral), I have survived the need for formal codification to define my professional behavior. Perhaps it was my experiences as a young nurse in watching the top obstetrician (who had taken the Hippocratic oath) in the city in which I was working perform an incompetent, unsterile delivery and receiving warnings from a coterie of young attending resident and internists (who also took that same oath) not to open my mouth regardless of what I saw. There I learned the dilemma of oaths and real life, of competence serving incompetence, of those with little power serving the powerful rather than the patient (the person whom we all had sworn an oath to protect), and of the patient so objectified that she and her baby became a part of the furniture in the delivery room. My experiences reminded me of *Boys in White* (Becker, Geer, Hughes, and Strauss, 1961), a book that documents how the medical school takes eager, altruistic young persons wanting to serve humanity and molds them into clever, and at times avaricious, professionals who desire status and money and in return lose their calling. This linking of professionalism with ethics and codes is absurd. Professionalism has the potential of being as disabling as it is enabling (Carlson, 1988; McKnight, 1977).

One could argue that my experiences as a young student nurse were isolated incidents, and that I should not be so cynical. Let me continue. I spent over ten years as an altruistic educator of leaders of youth within an interdenominational organization serving churches. My responsibility was to train women to be leaders of girls in a weekly club and summer camp format. If I learned not to trust the health industry, surely, within a church, an institution charged with the responsibility for providing oughts, I should have experienced the highest form of ethical behavior. What I experienced was sexism and racism.

First, the hundreds of women leaders with whom I was in contact made me realize that not only did they not expect themselves to be leaders or "all that they could be" but neither did the church or society. Woman after woman would say, when asked to take leadership, "Oh I can't do that, I'm just a housewife," and then with encouragement each would go on and become an outstanding leader. Why did women experience homemaking as a job not requiring leadership? When together we would deconstruct homemaking to see the complexities of the task, the women homemakers would be surprised; then we could easily demonstrate how those same skills transferred to leadership within the church and community.

But when the women began to utilize their leadership to challenge sexism within the church, both they and I were in "hot water." Further, when I became proactive in bringing African American and Caucasian leadership and girls together, when I actively developed the weekly club within churches serving nonwhites, I was in deeper hot water. As my boss told me, "Everytime we put a picture of a black camper in our journal, five churches cancel our program," and "If women in our educational programs start changing things in their church, the pastors begin to question having such a program; we have to be realistic." Accordingly, being realistic and having a successful adult training program meant promoting inequality, fostering injustice, and treating adult learners (and the girls that they taught) unethically. Would a code of ethics have changed this situation? No, I believe it would have only busied me with details such as shared decision processes in program planning and needs assessment, thus preventing me from seeing the bigger issues.

My flight to graduate school was a response to this revelation of the destructive nature of the traditional church, whose ethical code of "We are all priests after the order of Melchizedek" really meant "We white males who are the real priests will be the Melchizedek gatekeepers for you who are female and you who are black." After experiencing six years of graduate school, I finally got the picture. Medicine and the health field, the church and religious organizations, and education and its professional groups all had their codes, and these codes had very little to do with their everyday behavior. Persons involved were good people, good citizens as long as there were no changes in power relations affecting them. And as Kozol (1975) has so cogently described, many professionals, even those espousing or analyzing ethical behavior, found ways to critique but not promote any change if it meant confrontation or even sanctions.

While I was in graduate school, the Vietnam War, the civil rights movement, and the countercultural revolution came to a head. The young adults taught me, who had only experienced the "good war" (World War II), that there were other kinds of war; ordinary black citizens taught me that not they but rather the racist structures in our society were the problem; young undergraduate women taught me how serious is the gender bias in our society. The unassigned books that I read outside of class taught me about imperialism, classism, and the effects of cultural hegemony. Why did I have to learn this avocationally, at the protests, at the sit-ins, on the street, in the books not on our reading lists? I was at the time a full-time graduate student learning to "push back the frontiers of knowledge." Why did the university not give tenure to those professors who appeared to be the brightest, the most interested, the most unselfish, and the most involved in making the world a better place for all people? Intrigued with Kohlberg's (1958) formulation, I wrote my first dissertation proposal on the lack of moral behavior in adult educators. This is when I consciously knew that ethical behavior cannot be legislated. Institutions and ideological apparatus are developed by society to keep everything in place—they are there for social control. To make sure things do not change, we implicitly or explicitly develop codes to control behavior so that the social structure is affirmed. This is why we can, as Carlson (1988) so clearly pointed out, develop ethical principles involving our craft at the technical level but lose sight of a more basic and comprehensive ethic.

Justification of My View

McKnight (1977) has spoken of the disabling professions; Thompson (1980) and her colleagues discuss mystification as part of professionalism. Professionalism is associated with a code of ethics, yet "need-generating" professionals appear to generate client needs primarily to serve their own needs. How is adult education any different from that delivery room I experienced as a young nurse forty-five years ago? Look at the deficiency discourse of basic education, the mandated continuing professional education for professionals, the erosion of the education of adults in voluntary agencies, the growth of adult education as schooling, the vocationalization of the field with technical rationality in the driver's seat. Meanwhile, as the marketplace drives the profession, who makes the rules? Who wins? Who loses? Whose codes legitimate whose practices? Whose ideology is protected by whose hegemony? According to Collins (1991), a more appropriate approach may be the "ideal discourse" posited by Habermas in which a normative discourse is negotiated by all participants and in which all come to the table with equal power to make decisions. This approach is at least democratic.

Normative behavior must be contextualized to prevent the concepts of the good, the true, and the beautiful from becoming so abstract that they lose all meaning. When contextualized, decision making on what ought to be done can be pursued democratically and critically. This contextualization ensures that our action and our rhetoric are combined in praxis, and it allows our oughts to be reexamined in time so that history informs the present but also allows us to *make history* by positing new social relationships. If these ethical decisions are made democratically, then the rules made by those in power can be confronted by those who are affected by our ethical decisions.

Senator Patrick Moynihan may believe from his present position of power that the most ethical policy is to force all persons on welfare, whose children are at least six months' old, to participate in education, and that the role of adult educators is to teach these adults the value of work

(Sheared, 1992). The adult receiving welfare may understand the value of work better than does Moynihan; in fact, the point that homemaking is work may have escaped Moynihan's notice. Moynihan has never had to care for a family with limited funds; he has never had to do paid housework and raise other people's children while having to leave one's own; he has never known what it is like to work for minimum wages and recognize that regardless of educational level one will likely never have the good life seen every night on television. Why not get a discussion going about the value of education and the value of work where everyone's voices can be heard? We might hear some very different views on the value of education. And we might generate an ethical concern regarding the adult educator's role in the JOBS program based not just on what the political elite think but on what those on welfare have to say.

Those wanting a code of ethics base their arguments on professionalism and the need for adult educators to police their own ranks. Connelly and Light (1991) even suggest that the Commission of Professors of Adult Education (CPAE) is the appropriate group to establish a code of ethics. As the current chair of CPAE, I say that what we in CPAE know best is what we do in universities. Universities foster an elitist position, and CPAE stands guard over the higher education knowledge base. It seems very unlikely that professors will design and enforce a code that changes who has power over knowledge.

Connelly and Light (1991) argue that social responsibility should be the first principle of a code of ethics and that adult educators should take leadership in demonstrating that the professions are not the private property of professionals but rather belong to society. They then augment that position by arguing for "inclusive philosophy" and "pluralism."

It is not clear to me how one can have one's cake here and eat it too. Professionalism is defined by intellectual elitism (those that know against those who do not), knowledge guardianship (an official body of knowledge), technology (training for predictable problems that suggests decontextualization of knowledge and objectivity), altruism (benevolence for the public and service from the professional), and self-regulation (professionals call foul play, if necessary, on their buddies). We could develop a code, but there would be no outside voices by definition.

Professionalization is not about social change and never will be; to suggest that "inclusive philosophy" is like a "philosoteria" where the same adult educator uses "behaviorism" one hour and "radicalism" the next seems unrealistic to me; and professionalism cannot be defined by diversity but rather only by monopoly and homogenization. The term *diversity* used in this way means a narrow band of behaviors as well as a control of attitude. When John Ohliger spoke out on mandatory continuing education and, on principle, resigned his tenured full professorship at Ohio State University, he was punished by many, if not most, in the professoriate, who either ignored him or acted directly against him. I heard one of the most revered leaders in our profession say, "He made his bed, let him lie in it." This was an interesting response to professionally guaranteed academic freedom. And this is only one example. One can document the problems of such giants in the field as Jonathan Kozol, Myles Horton, and Paulo Freire, and also the less well known, such as George Van der Loos (Ohliger, 1989), who lost his job in an Alberta, Canada, community college because he opposed competence-based education.

The Better Way

Adult continuing educators should be concerned about ethics because all responsible citizens in a society need to have that concern. After all, societies are merely groups of people with an agreed-on set of social relations who live within the social structures and culture generated by that interaction. My one ought is to develop an environment for critical reflection in which I, as but a single participant without privilege, say what ought to be.

How can I do this? Here is my response today. I will not rely on technology (andragogy, needs assessment, evaluation, curriculum content, program planning models) but will continually examine it for its appropriateness. I will try to be open to new arguments and hear criticism of my standpoints. I will encourage participatory planning, implementation, evaluation, and decision making. I will try not to hide behind professionalism. I will seek out opinions and standpoints in opposition to mine. My ethical decisions will be contextually derived and informed by all of those involved.

References

Becker, H., Geer, B., Hughes, E., and Strauss, A. *Boys in White.* Chicago: University of Chicago Press, 1961.

Carlson, R. A. "A Code of Ethics for Adult Educators?" In R. G. Brockett (ed.), *Ethical Issues in Adult Education.* New York: Teachers College Press, 1988.

Collins, M. *Adult Education as Vocation.* New York: Routledge & Kegan Paul, 1991.

Connelly, R. J., and Light, K. M. "An Interdisciplinary Code of Ethics for Adult Education." *Adult Education Quarterly,* 1991, *41* (4), 233–240.

Kohlberg, L. "The Development of Modes of Moral Thinking and Choice in the Years 10 to 16." Unpublished doctoral dissertation, University of Chicago, 1958.

Kozol, J. *The Night Is Dark and I Am Far from Home.* New York: Simon & Schuster, 1975.

McKnight, J. "Professionalized Service and Disabling Help." In I. Illich (ed.), *Disabling Professions.* London, England: Marion Boyars, 1977.

Ohliger, J. "Dead Poets Society Seen in Life." *Adult and Continuing Education Today,* 1989, *19* (19), 6.

Sheared, V. "From Workfare to Edfare: The JOBS Program and African American Women." Unpublished doctoral dissertation, Department of Leadership and Educational Policy Studies, Northern Illinois University, 1992.

Thompson, J. (ed.). *Adult Education for a Change.* London, England: Hutchinson, 1980.

PHYLLIS M. CUNNINGHAM is a scholar activist at Northern Illinois University, De Kalb, who has a concern for ethical behavior that leads to democratic social change. Toward those goals, she is actively involved with Basic Choices, Inc., North American Popular Educators: Working Together for Social Change, and the International Council for Adult Education.

The development of a code of ethics is an obligation of any group of professionals whose actions may cause harm to those who are served, and adult and continuing education can be a harmful activity.

Adult and Continuing Education Needs a Code of Ethics

Thomas J. Sork, Brenda A. Welock

We take the position that adult education is obliged to develop a code of ethics. In one respect, the question of whether adult education should develop a code of ethics is moot since one code for adult and community educators is already in draft form and another is being considered by those in continuing higher education. But, in another respect, the question is still important because if the dangers of developing a code are indeed substantial, then those who are in the process of doing so should be forewarned. We begin our argument in favor of a code of ethics by identifying flaws in the arguments against our position.

Flaws in Arguments Against Developing a Code

We have become convinced of the desirability of developing a code of ethics, in part, by looking carefully at the arguments that have been put forward against these codes, arguments that we believe are flawed. These arguments fail to convince because they are based on (1) unwarranted assumptions, (2) overly narrow views of the purposes of adult education, (3) biased perspectives on the "evils" of professionalization, (4) mistaken notions of what constitutes a code of ethics, or (5) unreasonable fears that a code of ethics would somehow restrict entry to the field, reduce diversity of opportunities, and otherwise constrain those who are committed to providing adult education programs.

Unwarranted Assumptions. One unwarranted assumption is that the practice of adult education is so diverse that a code of ethics would be either far too vague or else relevant to only a small portion of the field.

This assumption has been challenged by Connelly and Light (1991), who argue that the pluralism of the field is one of its important strengths and that it is quite feasible to develop an interdisciplinary code of ethics that acknowledges and celebrates this diversity.

Another assumption is that adult educators neither want nor need a code of ethics, that they are quite content with the status quo and feel that other forces will protect adult learners from harm. McDonald (1991) surveyed attitudes regarding the need for a code of ethics to guide practice among three groups of adult educators in Indiana. She found that "the majority of Indiana adult basic educators, American Society for Training and Development members within Indiana, and the Indiana Council for Continuing Education believe there should be a code of ethics for them as adult educators" (1991, p. 1). There has been no other large-scale survey to determine practitioners' views on the desirability of a code of ethics, but calls for the development of a code of ethics issued by adult education scholars (Boulmetis and Russo, 1991; Griffith, 1991; Connelly and Light, 1991) and efforts by various professional associations to develop codes of ethics (Michigan Adult and Community Educators, 1992; P. A. Lawler, personal communication, December 1991) provide clear evidence of support. Related efforts to develop methods to guide ethical problem solving in adult education provide further evidence of concern about dealing more directly and effectively with the inevitable ethical issues that confront practitioners (Brockett, 1990; Lawler and Fielder, 1991; Sork, 1987).

Narrow View of Purposes. Adult education has many legitimate and important purposes, including empowerment of learners, increased competence of those who work and live in a rapidly changing society, promotion of critical thinking, and facilitation of adult learning. Those who believe that adult education should have only one purpose may rightly be fearful of a code of ethics because its development within such a diverse field would implicitly acknowledge the legitimacy of multiple purposes. To be useful, a code of ethics would have to take into account the wide range of settings in which adult education occurs, the wide range of purposes that it is used to achieve, and the diverse ideologies and philosophical frames that guide the work of its practitioners. Acknowledgment of this diversity in a document as public as a code of ethics would weaken the arguments of those who promote a one-dimensional view of the purpose of adult education.

Evils of Professionalization. There is general consensus that development of a code of ethics is an important step in professionalizing an occupation. Carlson (1988), among others, has argued that professionalization is, on balance, an undesirable development in any occupation because it leads to abuse of privilege and to the adoption of codes designed more to protect the special interests of the professional than the interests of those served by the professional. There are indeed evils of professionalization, but it is erroneous to conclude either that these evils are inevitable or that, on balance, they outweigh the benefits of professionalization. Examples of ethical shortcomings of practitioners in law and medicine are often used by critics to illustrate the pitfalls of professionalization, but these professions are simply not good models for adult education. The character of the services that they provide is different, as is the degree of autonomy of practitioners, the dependence of the client on the practitioner, and the degree of control over entry into practice. Critics also seem to assume that the road to professionalization followed by law and medicine is the only road available to adult education and that this road will inevitably lead to the same shortcomings. We believe, as do others such as Cervero (1987), that the professionalization of adult education should take and is taking a very different road—one built with full awareness of the pitfalls experienced by other professions, with great sensitivity to the character of the practitioner-client relationship, and with commitment to avoid the abuses of professional status evident in other professions.

Mistaken Notions of What Constitutes a Code of Ethics. There has been legitimate criticism of some of the documents that have been either presented or interpreted as codes of ethics, such as the *Principles of Good Practice in Continuing Education,* published by the Council on the Continuing Education Unit (1984). This document was designed to set standards of practice but has been interpreted by some as a rudimentary code of ethics. Carlson (1988) mistakenly uses the document as a surrogate for a code in what is generally a good discussion of the potential pitfalls of developing a code in adult education. Yet, the document is not even a rudimentary code of ethics because it does not directly deal with values or philosophical principles but instead focuses on procedures. Carlson and other critics of the *Principles of Good Practice in Continuing Education* (Mezirow, 1984) have rightly taken issue with the implicit values of the procedures and observe that these do not in any way represent shared values of the field. A true code of ethics deals *explicitly* with shared values and the implications for practice of accepting those values.

Fears That a Code of Ethics Will Be Restrictive. By themselves, codes of ethics place no constraints at all on practice. It is how codes are used and misused by groups who develop and administer them that may make them restrictive. For example, if a professional association develops a code and requires its members to adhere to the code or risk expulsion from the association, then the code becomes a tool to restrict membership. And if membership in the association is a prerequisite to practice, then the code is also a tool to restrict entry to practice. But the development of a code does not inevitably lead to restrictive uses. Some codes are used only as guides to help practitioners make more informed decisions when they confront ethical dilemmas or conflicts of values in their work. Others are used only to communicate the shared values of members of an organization to those who may wish to join. So restrictive uses of codes are possible but not inevitable; in a field that values democratic participation in decision making, it seems unlikely that a code would be used to restrict practice unless it was with the approval of those involved in the process.

Consequences of Not Developing a Code

Because arguments against development of a code of ethics are unnecessarily negative and contain fatal flaws, and in light of the fact that codes of ethics for adult education are already being drafted, all indicators point to the need to proceed with the development of a code of ethics that incorporates both the collective experience of adult education practitioners (case specifics related to the field) and the philosophical bases that necessarily ground a code in the ethical dimension of practice (general guiding principles and ethical theories). The consequences of *not* developing a code are costly. We contend that if the field does nothing to sensitize its practitioners to the ethical consequences of their actions, then the integrity of the field will be jeopardized "because nothing bankrupts credibility more promptly than suspicion of ethical dereliction" (Walker, 1983, p. 207). A code of ethics for adult education would substantially reduce reliance on the marketplace or individual morality to control unethical practices and would place this responsibility within its rightful domain—the adult education community. Additional evidence of a concern with the moral dimension of practice is the recent adoption of *A Bill of Rights for the Adult Learner* by the Coalition of Adult Education Organizations (1991). The twelve learners' rights contained in this document suggest a corresponding set of professional obligations for those who develop and offer programs. It is doubtful that this type of document would have been developed and adopted if individual morality or the marketplace were sufficient to prevent the abuse of the rights of adult learners.

The "public impression of adult educators as merchandisers who are available to promote the ideas, as well as the values, of others, but who have no professional values of their own" (Griffith, 1991) needs to be corrected. The practice of relying solely on individual morality or the marketplace is indeed dangerous and will have serious consequences if continued. If individual morality alone was enough to guide practice, then we would not be embroiled in this discussion in the first place because there would be no instances of ethically questionable practices. Individual morality is subjective and relates to personal responsibility. It does not necessarily include consideration of others, nor can it be relied on to produce consistent actions. North American adult educators are members of a pluralistic society in which individuals receive moral guidance from many diverse sources. We believe that the diversity of moral convictions, coupled with external pressures for expedient decisions, is responsible for the inconsistency seen in adult education practices, and that it supplies evidence of the need for ethical guidance. The action orientation of the field focuses the practitioner on the pragmatic assessment of what works rather than on the philosophical question of what should be (Monette, 1979). A code of ethics would provide the necessary guidance for ethical practice, exemplifying what the field as a whole considers right, wrong, or obligatory based on core values. It could unite the field by supplying a philosophical perspective that transcends the institutional barriers that prevent many practitioners from identifying with the adult education community.

Not only has individual morality failed to safeguard the public, but the marketplace has been even less successful. It is likely that in some cases it has even encouraged unethical practices by providing financial rewards for programs high in inspiration and low in substance. Assurance of participation in programs may take precedence over educational quality in a cost-recovery or profit-motivated organization. A short-term profit orientation will eventually lead us away from our long-term commitment to provide learning opportunities for adults in all socioeconomic circumstances throughout their life spans.

Two recent cases reported in the press illustrate the problem of relying on either individual morality or the marketplace to provide safeguards. The Miami case (Henriques, 1991) is an example of the failure of both individual morality and the marketplace to regulate ethical practice, and it demonstrates the kind of legal intervention that we can expect in the future if the field does not take on the task of self-regulation. In this case, both the instructor of a course on investments and the school district through which the course was offered are being sued. The plaintiffs, who were all students in the course, allege that the instructor, who was also a stockbroker, used his professional status to gain the confidence of the adult learners to further his own self-interests and used the classroom as a forum to increase his client base. Those from the course who became clients of the broker lost heavily on investments that he recommended. In the Edmonton case (Jeffs, 1991), the Canadian province of Alberta paid $1,000 for an illiterate single mother to attend a two-week job search program. Part of the program involved the preparation of a resume, which, in the case of this particular woman, contained a list of skills that overstated her qualifications. According to the story, "The resume says she can 'operate cash registers efficiently' and is 'familiar with all types of flowers, plants, and how to feed and water correctly,' but [the woman] said she's never operated a register in her life and doesn't know anything about plant care" (Jeffs, 1991, p. A7). Although an obvious embarrassment to the government, the story is, more important, an illustration of the ethical shortcomings of a system in which the financial interests of the instructor or the agency providing the course carry more weight than do the interests of the learner and of the taxpayers who support the program.

The field of adult education is experiencing an identity crisis as the size of our membership increases. When we identify ourselves to the public as adult educators, it should tell them something about what we do, what they can expect from the services that we provide, and what ideals guide our practice. Clearly, the time has come for the adult education community to assume a leadership role in reducing the probability of ethical transgressions, or surely some outside regulatory organization will step in to fill this void. Although some might argue that adult education is an emerging field and lacks the maturity necessary to develop a useful code of ethics (Singarella and Sork, 1983), this argument was much more convincing thirty, twenty, or even ten years ago than it is today. Adult education has in fact already emerged and can no longer avoid its ethical responsibilities by relying on arguments that it lacks the maturity needed or is too diverse to develop a code of ethics.

Benefits of Developing a Code of Ethics

The benefits of developing a code of ethics can be easily identified. First, it will provide a tool that practitioners can use to guide them away from ethically hazardous practices. An ethically hazardous practice is an action or decision that may be inconsistent with one of the values reflected in the code or that violates one of the principles included in the code. Second, a code will provide direction to adult education organizations and agencies in policy-making. Codes of ethics and policies based on them do not guarantee ethical practice, but policies that are consistent with the core values reflected in a code will reinforce the idea that the provider stands for certain values and attempts to operate in a manner consistent with those values. Third, a code will provide limited protection from unethical practice for adult learners, although the degree of protection afforded by a code will depend on how the code is used. Adult education providers who adopt the code as more than just a marketing device will presumably act to ensure that their practices are consistent with the code. A code will provide criteria that learners can use if they wish to challenge the way that they are treated.

Fourth, a code can be used in professional preparation programs for adult educators to better communicate the shared values of those in the field. Spirited discussion and debate about these values should be a part of every program that purports to prepare reflective practitioners who understand the philosophical basis of their work and who are guided in this work by a consistent set of values. Fifth, a code will raise the visibility of the moral dimension of practice. It is easy to fall into the trap of viewing adult education as largely a values-neutral or ethically benign technical process of arranging for instructors, classrooms, materials, publicity, registrations, and so on. The process of developing a code would lay to rest this mistaken notion and would force those in the field to come to terms with the harm as well as the benefits that can result from their work. And, finally, a code will provide a means of differentiating among providers. If an agency decided to adopt the code and to be held accountable to the code by its clients, the agency can use that commitment to set itself apart from others who do not make this kind of commitment.

Our view is that these and other benefits from the careful development of a code of ethics for adult education far outweigh potential problems that may develop. There is no doubt that the tasks of developing a code of ethics and gaining its acceptance will be challenging. But we believe that with knowledge of the problems that other professions have encountered in developing and using a code, a commitment to a highly participatory and democratic process of code development, thoughtful application of the code, and a willingness to acknowledge weaknesses in the code and to change it when needed, the field of adult education can advance substantially. It will be a code that is based on the best of what our field has to offer and on a set of shared values that celebrates human potential and democratic ideals.

In supporting the position that adult education should develop a code of ethics, Connelly and Light (1991, p. 238) observe that "a code of ethics in itself, of course, cannot guarantee ethical practice or be a cure-all for other problems in a profession. To have such expectations is to mistake the main purpose of a code. A code of ethics speaks to the very best that a profession is or strives to be. It is not a list of standards or minimum competencies. It is the idealistic side of a profession, a projection of the vision of professional identity as it ought to be." Adult education is ready to develop this vision of professional identity. The question of whether adult education should develop a code of ethics is no longer relevant. The relevant question is how to best get on with the task.

References

Boulmetis, J., and Russo, F. X. "A Question of Ethics." *Community Education Journal,* 1991, *18* (2), 15–18.

Brockett, R. G. "Adult Education: Are We Doing It Ethically?" *Journal of Adult Education,* 1990, *19* (1), 5–12.

Carlson, R. A. "A Code of Ethics for Adult Educators?" In R. G. Brockett (ed.), *Ethical Issues in Adult Education.* New York: Teachers College Press, 1988.

Cervero, R. M. "Professionalization as an Issue for Continuing Education." In R. G. Brockett (ed.), *Continuing Education in the Year 2000.* New Directions for Adult and Continuing Education, no. 36. San Francisco: Jossey-Bass, 1987.

Coalition of Adult Education Organizations. *A Bill of Rights for the Adult Learner.* Washington, D.C.: Coalition of Adult Education Organizations, 1991. (Available from David W. Stewart, Director of Program Development, American Council on Education, One Dupont Circle, Washington, DC 20036-1193.)

Connelly, R. J., and Light, K. M. "An Interdisciplinary Code of Ethics for Adult Education." *Adult Education Quarterly,* 1991, *41* (4), 233–240.

Council on the Continuing Education Unit. *Principles of Good Practice in Continuing Education*. Silver Spring, Md.: Council on the Continuing Education Unit, 1984.

Griffith, W. S. "Do Adult Educators Need a Code of Ethics?" *Adult Learning*, 1991, 2 (8), 4.

Henriques, D. B. "Students in a Class on Investments Say the Lessons Meant Big Losses." *New York Times*, May 26, 1991, pp. A1, A26. (Reprinted in *Adult and Continuing Education Today*, 1991, 21 (23), 1-2, 5-6.)

Jeffs, A. "Resume Created by Job Program Is Phoney, Woman Says." *Edmonton Journal*, Aug. 28, 1991, p. A7.

Lawler, P. A., and Fielder, J. H. "Analyzing Ethical Problems in Continuing Higher Education: A Model for Practical Use." *Journal of Continuing Higher Education*, 1991, 39 (2), 20-24.

McDonald, K. S. "A Study of the Attitudes of Adult Education Practitioners About Codes of Ethics." Unpublished doctoral dissertation, Department of Educational Leadership, Ball State University, 1991.

Mezirow, J. "Review of *Principles of Good Practice in Continuing Education*." *Lifelong Learning: An Omnibus of Practice and Research*, 1984, 8 (3), 27-28, 30.

Michigan Adult and Community Educators. Ethics Committee. *Adult and Community Education Professional Code of Ethics*. Orchard Lake: Michigan Adult and Community Educators, 1992.

Monette, M. L. "Needs Assessment: A Critique of Philosophical Assumptions." *Adult Education*, 1979, 29, 83-95.

Singarella, T. A., and Sork, T. J. "Questions of Values and Conduct: Ethical Issues for Adult Education." *Adult Education Quarterly*, 1983, 33, 244-251.

Sork, T. J. "Ethics and Actions." In C. Klevins (ed.), *Materials and Methods in Adult and Continuing Education*. Los Angeles: Kelvens, 1987.

Walker, D. E. "Ethical Suspicions of Faculty and Administrators." In M. C. Baca and R. H. Stein (eds.), *Ethical Practices and Problems in Higher Education*. Springfield, Ill.: Thomas, 1983.

THOMAS J. SORK is associate professor of adult education at the University of British Columbia, Vancouver, British Columbia, Canada. He has a longstanding interest in the ethics of practice.

BRENDA A. WELOCK is a programmer in the Department of Community Programs and Services at Douglas College, New Westminster, British Columbia.

PART SEVEN

Should Adult and Continuing Education Professionals Be Certified?

Certification is neither feasible nor realistic for the field of adult and continuing education because of the diversity and lack of stability of the field.

Professional Certification Is Not Needed in Adult and Continuing Education

Waynne Blue James

More than ten years ago, I argued against certification on the grounds that it is neither a feasible nor a necessary process for the field of adult education (James, 1981). Although several individuals or institutions have more recently confronted the issue, no one has been able to suggest a single certification process that covers the entire field. Cynicism about the development of an adequate process is still appropriate for many of the same reasons. The range of diversity within the field is so great that it is impossible to develop a certification system for all of the entities within the domain of adult education. At the same time, the lack of stability within the field also obstructs the creation of a comprehensive certification process.

Personal Viewpoint

To briefly summarize my original stance, I argued that five basic assumptions were not feasible or realistic for the field of adult education: a unique core of knowledge and skills can be identified for the entire field, the level of required competence can easily be established, a process and an entity to oversee the system for the entire field can be designed, certification offers recognition and protection for the field, and certification and teacher effectiveness are demonstrably interrelated. In the ensuing years since my original rebuttal of these five assumptions, different perspectives on the certification issue have been developed. However, I still believe that little has changed to make certification either practical or attainable for the entire field.

I must admit that when I first began formulating my argument in 1981,

NEW DIRECTIONS FOR ADULT AND CONTINUING EDUCATION, no. 54, Summer 1992 © Jossey-Bass Publishers

I was leaning a little more toward believing in the need and power of certification; however, as I gathered information and thought through the issue, I became convinced of the impossibility of implementing a workable, quality certification system. Since then, I have maintained my opposition to the development of a system of certification.

Recent Views and Criticism

Gilley and Galbraith, either singularly or together, have authored a series of articles, monographs, and research reports in support or clarification of professional certification (Galbraith, 1987; Galbraith and Gilley, 1985, 1986; Gilley, 1985; Gilley and Galbraith, 1987, 1988). Among other points, Galbraith and Gilley (1985) rightly contended that neither I nor Cameron (1981) specifically defined the term *certification*. They then proceeded to define a variety of terms often used interchangeably (certification, licensure, and accreditation). Professional certification was defined "as a voluntary process by which a professional association or organization measures the competencies of individual practitioners" (1985, p. 2). They distinguished professional certification from licensure, which was defined as "a mandatory process by which the government permits the individual to practice in designated professions" (p. 2). And accreditation was defined as "a voluntary process by which an independent agency grants recognition to an education program or institution" (p. 2).

Three components of professionalization and professional certification were identified in Gilley and Galbraith (1987). These components are level of knowledge and competence enhancement, level of importance of occupation to society, and level of control by members of the occupation. One need only consider these three components to see that the entire field of adult education is nowhere close to being able to implement a certification process. First, although it may be possible to identify the level of knowledge and competencies needed by adult educators, it is harder to convince the rest of society that the occupation is very important to society. Most K–12 educators do not enjoy the luxury of being perceived as a necessity by society (just consider the amount of influence that state legislatures have on education), so why should adult education be any different? Finally, related to the third component, at this time not only does adult education have *no* control over its own field but it seems unlikely that adult educators will have control anytime in the near future, if ever. We have no means to police our own field and no means to begin implementing a process of control.

Part of the reason for lack of control relates to the diversity and extensiveness of adult education activities. Some entities have been making attempts to certify specific areas of adult education, such as California's efforts in adult basic education and Canada's Certificate in Adult Education (CAE). California established a task force to review the issue of certification for adult basic education teachers. One of the task force statements was that "there is widespread agreement that credentialing and certification are important issues. However, there is little agreement about the need for credentialing and certification" (Miller, 1990, p. 21). The task force continued by stating that voluntary certification as a "means to enhance the profession is an empty claim as there is no evidence that enhancement does not improve the competence and performance of teachers" (p. 21). The Canadian CAE program was first established in 1971, and its effects have been evaluated through 1983. Stalker (1983, p. i) concluded that the CAE program has had a "small or rather insignificant impact [emphasis added] on the product, or the quality of instruction." She argues that successful implementation of the program would require "organizational leadership and a sound administrative structure" (p. 22). In other words, a strong, well-defined structure is crucial to the effectiveness and, thereby, success of any certification program.

Diversity of the Field

My current position is that many of the same issues that hindered certification more than a decade ago still exist. These issues include the inability of even a single entity to establish a system of certification, the failure to show that certification acts as a source of protection and recognition for the field of adult education, and the difficulty of establishing competence criteria for each of the subareas of specialization within degree programs in adult education.

The field of adult education has been viewed from several perspectives that illustrate its diversity. Schroeder (1970, 1980) presented his typology of institutions offering education opportunities for adults. Darkenwald and Merriam (1982) adapted his four types slightly, calling them independent adult educational agencies, educational institutions, quasi-educational organizations, and noneducational organizations. Apps (1989) presented a slightly different typology of the providers of adult education opportunities: fully or partially tax-supported institutions, nonprofit self-supporting institutions, for-profit providers, and nonorganized learning opportunities. This variety of entities providing adult education activities is so diverse that it is impossible to include them under one single certification system.

Added to the diversity of providers are the array of roles that individuals within the provider institutions must fill. The variety of roles and responsibilities are filled not only by teachers but also by administrators, supervisors, counselors, program developers, aides, and curriculum developers. There are full-time workers as well as part-time employees and volunteers. Any attempt to develop one system for all of the providers and all of the roles within the field is hopeless. It becomes easy to see that a single certification process is not possible, and attempts to develop multiple certification processes to cover each type of institution and role constitute an absurd strategy.

In continuing this line of inquiry, it is important to realize that practitioners have not yet established a totally accepted body of knowledge or identified a set of skills needed for each of the areas within the entire field. Without an accepted body of knowledge or an identified skills area, no professional credentialing or certification situation program can be established.

It is necessary to explore some of the following issues in considering a certification program. Is teaching adults in a business and industry setting any different from teaching adults in the public school system or through cooperative extension workshops? What differences exist? Each area would need to determine its own unique competencies on top of the core competencies. Moreover, who should certification serve? What basis should it include, and is there a difference in certification by the type of role or type of agency? Who should oversee the program?

Problems in establishing levels of competence are common to all competence-based programs. Who establishes the standards? At what level? Too high levels restrict admission, too low levels may admit individuals of questionable competence. One of my colleagues, opposed to competence-based education, has stated that minimum standards create low achievement and mediocrity because we are then striving for the minimum rather than the maximum. I think that he has a legitimate point.

Stability of the Field

Related to the diversity issues are the problems of stability within the various areas. Literacy programs are partially dependent on federal and state funds for operation. Businesses and industries often find that when economic times get tough, the training function is one of the first functions to be cut or eliminated. In addition to the funding concerns, the lack of a single professional entity to speak for the entire field is a crucial issue. Imel (1988, p. ii) wrote that "debate [related to certification] concerns determination of an appropriate credential and credentialing body." It is obvious to me that any single (or combined) association is incapable of serving as a credentialing body. Problems exist in relation to the prestige of the association, monetary concerns, turf conflicts, and the voluntary nature of professional associations.

Specifically related to the problem of the identification of a single entity are the hindrances related to the associations currently existing in the field of adult education. Having been rather intimately involved in the workings of the American Association for Adult and Continuing Education (AAACE), I know firsthand some of the problems that the association and the field face. The tenuous financial situation of AAACE and some of the other related associations is one of the key problems. The competition and turf battles experienced by associations with overlapping missions are another major hurdle.

Which associations actually serve the interests of adult learners? There is no one single association that speaks for all adult learners; rather, there is a variety of fragmented groups who tend to serve some needs of some adults. AAACE probably comes closest to serving the range of needs of most adult learners. All of the associations tend to want a part of the target audience of adults; this, in turn, leads to turf problems and to head-to-head competition in some cases. Which entity would best serve the needs of the field? Obviously, there is no easy answer to this question.

The voluntary nature of most associations creates a feeble base on which to build a strong system. While I was an active participant in the political structure of AAACE, I remember regularly hearing that "20 percent of the people in the association accomplish 80 percent of the work." From personal observation, I wholeheartedly agree with that statement. This is not to lay blame on individuals; rather, it is an acknowledgment of the voluntary nature of our associations. Most of the people who volunteer to serve an association also have a myriad of other responsibilities such as jobs, spouses, and children.

Implications

Galbraith and Gilley (1986) cite six areas of negative implications for professional certification programs: division among professionals and the professions, core competence identification, applicant evaluation, financial and human costs, membership restrictions, and regulation of the profession. Each of these areas can be directly tied to the diversity and lack of stability of the field of adult education. For example, the division of the field acerbates the conflict and identity problems that the various areas already possess. The issue of who can, or should, identify the core competencies again leads to direct competition between the various entities with vested interests in the matter. The lack of a single association that can speak for the entire field makes it impossible to develop measurable standards and a process of certification that will be acceptable to all entities concerned with adult education. I doubt that any one institution or agency would be able to handle the financial and human resources costs associated with the development of a system of certification. Restriction of membership or entry into the field becomes impossible unless there is one overall process of certification (and this does not even address the legal issue of excluding individuals); but, as I have already stated, one overall process is an impossibility. And, finally, since no single entity is capable of developing one overall system, no one is capable of serving as the regulatory agency for the system. Therefore, a comprehensive, thorough certification system is a preposterous proposal.

Although Gilley (1985) claimed that other professional associations have addressed the five assumptions that I stated earlier, there is truly no proof that they have successfully addressed the issues. The development of a professional certification program and the demonstration of its effectiveness are two different tasks. Galbraith and Gilley (1985, p. 14) can make distinctions between "those who are qualified and those who are not." If there is no proof that certification ensures effective teachers, how can such a complicated, unwieldy process be worth the effort, energy, time, and resources? Cope and others (1983), Miller (1990), and Stalker (1983) all claim that there is no evidence or proof that certification is linked to effective practice. One might also suggest that there is no proof for any of the other variables or dimensions purportedly related to effective practice in adult education. Nor is there any evidence that other possible roles within the field are positively affected.

Relationship to Practice

Certification is not only impractical but also unattainable for the entire field and, therefore, should not be implemented on a large-scale basis. Within certain specific and select areas of the field, however, certification may be a possibility. There may be some benefit to adding a certification area to public school teachers' and administrators' certificates for literacy programs (adult basic education or general educational development), but this is a narrow portion of the field representing only one type of agency.

Do I believe today that certification is a possible benefit to professionalizing adult education? Probably. Do I believe that the process of certification is any more feasible today than it was ten years ago? Definitely not. As an optimist, I would like to believe that there are ways to enhance the professionalism of the field. I have spent many years of my professional career providing service and leadership to the national association to help achieve the goal of enhanced professionalism. Although I have a great love for the field, I am also realistic enough to know that, at this particular point in history, we are neither defined enough, strong enough, secure enough, nor respected enough to be able to establish a workable, beneficial certification process.

Certification demands an intricate, systematized process. It should be obvious that the development of that intricate, systematized process is beyond the capacity of adult educators today.

References

Apps, J. W. "Providers of Adult and Continuing Education: A Framework." In S. B. Merriam and P. M. Cunningham (eds.), *Handbook of Adult and Continuing Education*. San Francisco: Jossey-Bass, 1989.

Cameron, C. "Certification Should Be Established." In B. W. Kreitlow and Associates, *Examining Controversies in Adult Education*. San Francisco: Jossey-Bass, 1981.

Cope, J. L., and others. *Feasibility of Requiring and Delivering Certification for ABE Teachers in Pennsylvania*. Indiana: Indiana University of Pennsylvania, 1983.

Darkenwald, G. G., and Merriam, S. B. *Adult Education: Foundations of Practice*. New York: HarperCollins, 1982.

Galbraith, M. W. "Certification Would Advance Professional Practice." *Lifelong Learning: An Omnibus of Practice and Research*, 1987, *11* (2), 15, 18.

Galbraith, M. W., and Gilley, J. W. "An Examination of Professional Certification." *Lifelong Learning: An Omnibus of Practice and Research*, 1985, *9* (2), 12-15.

Galbraith, M. W., and Gilley, J. W. *Professional Certification: Implications for Adult Education and HRD*. Columbus, Ohio: ERIC Clearinghouse on Adult, Career, and Vocational Education, 1986.

Gilley, J. W. "Professional Certification: The Procedures Established, the Issues Addressed, and the Qualification Criteria Adopted by Professional Associations and Societies." Unpublished doctoral dissertation, Department of Occupational and Adult Education, Oklahoma State University, 1985.

Gilley, J. W., and Galbraith, M. W. "Professionalization and Professional Certification: A Relationship." In *Proceedings of the 28th Annual Adult Education Research Conference*. Laramie: University of Wyoming, 1987.

Gilley, J. W., and Galbraith, M. W. "Commonalities and Characteristics of Professional Certification: Implications for Adult Education." *Lifelong Learning: An Omnibus of Practice and Research*, 1988, *12* (1), 11-14, 17.

Imel, S. *Trends and Issues in Adult Education*. Columbus, Ohio: Clearinghouse on Adult, Career, and Vocational Education, 1988.

James, W. B. "Certification Is Unfeasible and Unnecessary." In B. W. Kreitlow and Associates, *Examining Controversies in Adult Education*. San Francisco: Jossey-Bass, 1981.

Miller, C. *Teacher Certification Appropriate to Adult Education*. Sacramento: California State Department of Education, 1990.

Schroeder, W. L. "Adult Education Defined and Described." In R. M. Smith, G. F. Aker, and J. R. Kidd (eds.), *Handbook of Adult Education*. New York: Macmillan, 1970.

Schroeder, W. L. "Typology of Adult Learning Systems." In J. M. Peters and Associates, *Building an Effective Adult Education Enterprise*. San Francisco: Jossey-Bass, 1980.

Stalker, J. "Historical Study of the Certificate in Adult Education in Quebec." Unpublished Ed.D. practicum, Program in Higher Education, Nova University, 1983.

WAYNNE BLUE JAMES *is professor and coordinator of adult education at the University of South Florida, Tampa.*

Adult and continuing education should meet society's expectation for demonstrated professionalism by implementing options for professional certification.

Professional Certification Is a Needed Option for Adult and Continuing Education

Barbara A. White

As we prepare to enter the twenty-first century, society expects professionals from all disciplines to demonstrate competence in the roles played and tasks performed. My observations over the past twenty years lead me to believe that, in the field of adult education, societal expectations have moved from a context in which clients assumed that the professional had answers and could demonstrate appropriate skills to a context in which proof of competence is exacted prior to the investment of time, money, and energy. From my perspective, this proof does not necessarily mean the acquisition of an additional academic degree, but it may constitute any number of experiences and interactions providing a base from which the professional can maintain proficiency and competence in practice. One avenue for meeting these societal expectations is through the provision of a professional certification process that allows professionals the option of self-improvement and development.

The stated need for, and interest in, professional certification is not a recent issue within the field of adult and continuing education. Cameron (1981, p. 3), for example, presents a case for professional certification by suggesting that the changing tasks and continuing need for creativity and expansion of knowledge require a trained and qualified group of professionals: "Tasks of adult educators today are interwoven with the social and economic stability of our society and those of developing nations." Galbraith (1987) provides a different perspective in suggesting that professional certification is an enhancement to the field; in combination, the public and the discipline can make distinctions between those who demonstrate a specific expertise and those who do not.

As we move toward the year 2000, the debate centers on the need for a process that verifies that adult educators do indeed possess unique competencies in their individual educational practice, enabling them to meet the changing needs of society. Certainly, futurists of the 1990s predict an increasing demand for more and better prepared professionals and scholars; there will also be a greater demand for specialization, with employers and clientele expecting professionals to possess site-specific expertise in addition to core skills. In response to these predictions and to more traditional concerns, including protection of the public from incompetent practitioners, professional certification emerges as a viable solution.

Galbraith and Gilley (1986, p. 3) define professional certification as a "voluntary process regulated by the profession itself." Professional certification is distinguishable from other credentialing processes such as accreditation and licensure by its voluntary nature and regulation by a professional association or organization. Licensure and certification are considered mandated credentialing processes and are usually administered by state government or a political body (Galbraith and Gilley, 1985). The primary purpose of professional certification is to "promote the professional competencies of the association and society's membership" (Galbraith and Gilley, 1986, p. 5); the intent is not to restrict entrance into the profession but rather to advance the competencies of individual practitioners.

My position is that the crux of the certification issue lies not only in the end to acquire additional skills and knowledge to demonstrate competence but also, and more important, in the motivation underlying the demonstrated need to seek out those options. This motivation, in turn, may provide the necessary guarantee or confirmation to accommodate society's expectations. These motives "induce" the action to meet specific needs, whether internal or external, and may be guided by reactions to outside stimuli such as potential regulation by an association, anticipation of a negative consequence, control, or status. However, based on my observations of colleagues within the field and those representing other professions and associations, a higher-level motive must be in place: the motive of self-development or self-improvement.

How I Arrived at My Position on Certification

I concur with Galbraith and Gilley (1986) regarding the importance of professional certification as a means for promoting competencies within the field of adult and continuing education. In fact, taking this purpose one step further, it is my belief that a professional certification process can also provide standards by which our discipline can address the questions of who we are, what we are, and the level of proficiency that society should expect from its professionals representing a diversity of practice. However, it is the expectation of a level of proficiency that is central to my position.

For more than twenty years, I have worked within the framework of the university land grant system, which reflects a mission of teaching, research, and outreach. My exposure to professionals representing a variety of associations and professional organizations brings to mind continually a myriad of questions regarding accommodation of societal expectations for demonstrated expertise, decision making, and problem solving in real-life situations. One colleague, for example, in the professional association of home economics, suggested that, currently, a generic degree program, in combination with a certification program, is not a sufficient indicator to her clientele of proficiency in her area of specialization. The alternative of professional certification within the area of specialization, however, carries significantly more weight with the clientele.

A second example comes from a colleague who has provided insight into the future movement of the discipline of soil science toward professional certification. The expected need by the clientele for demonstrated accountability due to economic risk, in addition to the competitiveness of the marketplace, were just two of the reasons for consideration in the discipline of professional certification. Clientele do not perceive the basic qualifications of the degree program as indicators of competence and proficiency. A benefit of the professional certification process, as identified from a marketing standpoint, is that a certified soil scientist can provide a level of service that exceeds the competition. It is the interpretation of the discipline that "people in the know," such as leaders in the industry and individuals involved in the environmental arena, applaud professional certification as a logical cost-effective method for providing competent and proficient individuals.

In considering such a process, it is important that the field of adult education also review complementary disciplines and the lessons learned regarding professional certification. Cervero (1987) raises the question of what the field of continuing education should strive to become in the future, and he provides insight regarding the issues to be faced by educators. These include the question of what constitutes a profession, and, if identified as such, what model of professionalization should be used. Cervero's (1987, p. 71) suggestion that "professionals must be adequately trained and socialized so as to provide recognizably distinct services for exchange on the professional market" defines the dilemma currently faced by the field of adult education. He further suggests that difficulty exists for continuing education in the lack of ability to constitute and control a market for expertise in the specific subfields of practice. I have watched this same situation develop over the past years in the field of adult education as I interacted with professionals both in the academic and theory-based environment and in the practice field.

I agree with Brown (1984, p. 150) that "the occupation of adult education has an opportunity to develop an alternative model of professionalism
and that the challenge . . . is to develop an occupational model by sharing
power more equally between practitioner and client." Professional certification provides just such an opportunity by providing to the field of adult
education, through the various subfields of practice, an avenue for
enhanced professional development. The catalyst for the motive of self-
improvement or self-development may be societal and client expectations,
or it may be the educator's need for additional improvement to meet his or
her own individual professional expectations. Penland (1982) states the
premise well in the observation that associations that promote certification
as a means, not an end, and that emphasize quality on-the-job performance
can make valuable contributions.

It is my belief that the profession of adult education will need to assess societal expectations from a global perspective and, as a result, provide
alternatives through the various subfields within the profession that enable
educators to meet these expectations. The profession must design, develop,
and implement avenues of professional development, one of which is the
option of professional certification. With these opportunities available, the
adult educator must then take responsibility for his or her own self-improvement based on individual motives.

The fundamental concern of the field of adult education is not to
determine the best way to protect professional jobs or control entry into
the ranks. Educators work within the context of private business and industry, federal, state, and local agencies, city government, adult education via
the public school system, and so on. These individuals must have the
opportunity to build on their existing academic preparation, incorporating
the knowledge and skills from broad-based education into specific, credible
educational programs that utilize their expertise in the environments in
which they work and among those with whom they interact. As Brookfield
(1986, p. 287) suggests, "If we view effective practice solely as the improvement of ever more refined practice skills and regard facilitator roles and
responsibilities as being primarily those of technicians of design, we
denude practice of any philosophical rationale, future orientation, or pur-
poseful mission."

As we move through the 1990s, professionals must take into consideration societal concerns about matters other than individual technical
competencies; enhancement of the problem-solving and decision-making
expertise of on-site educators of adults through self-improvement and
self-development opportunities is also needed. As we must move forward
into the twenty-first century, educators of adults must be provided with
avenues to enhance and improve themselves professionally through certification programs.

Impact of Certification on the Profession

The question remains regarding the significance of the impact of professional certification on the field of adult and continuing education. I suggest that the motivation for professional certification will be both personal and professional. The process may serve to generate a customized career-long learning design or an individual curriculum for the highly motivated, self-directed learner. In addition, professional certification will provide other benefits, including the following:

First, the process will provide recognition for practitioners, which, in turn, may provide incentives for individuals to strive for levels of excellence that they may not have otherwise considered.

Second, standards will provide greater clarity to the field of adult education, as viewed by other specializations in which practitioners must interact (for example, legislative or government agencies and federal contracting agencies), many of whom have incorporated professional certification into their standards and expectations.

Third, professional certification will provide recognition to adult education practitioners who have obtained some qualifying level of competence in a specialized area, allowing the public and profession to make distinctions between those who are qualified and those who are not.

Fourth, from a broader perspective, professional certification will add credibility to existing programs by creating an awareness within society that adult education practitioners maintain a level of competence within specialized areas as well as a familiarity with the whole spectrum of the discipline.

Fifth, the process will provide an opportunity for a common core of knowledge and skills to be demonstrated by the adult educator, especially since the diverse needs of adult audiences require general as well as audience-specific backgrounds and expertise.

Sixth, the recognition of audience diversity by the practitioner can, in turn, serve the academic community as a feedback mechanism by ensuring that the appropriate skills and competencies are being developed by those individuals aspiring to practice in the field of adult education. In addition, this feedback can also confirm that current academic programs are developing competent professionals who will advance professional practice.

Seventh, professional certification will serve other ends such as promotion of professionalism, enhanced prestige of the adult education field, encouragement to remain in the profession, stability and individual job security, and perhaps even income enhancement.

As we enter the next century, the field of adult and continuing education should have addressed and determined the impact of professional certification. If conducted in a thoughtful and logical manner, the significance of professional certification on the profession and its members should be realized.

References

Brookfield, S. D. *Understanding and Facilitating Adult Learning: A Comprehensive Analysis of Principles and Effective Practices.* San Francisco: Jossey-Bass, 1986.

Brown, C. D. "Ideological Orientation and Attitudes Toward Professionalism Among Adult Educators." Unpublished doctoral dissertation, Department of Leadership and Educational Policy Studies, Northern Illinois University, 1984.

Cameron, C. R. "Certification Should Be Established." In B. W. Kreitlow and Associates, *Examining Controversies in Adult Education.* San Francisco: Jossey-Bass, 1981.

Cervero, R. M. "Professionalization as an Issue for Continuing Education." In R. G. Brockett (ed.), *Continuing Education in the Year 2000.* New Directions for Adult and Continuing Education, no. 36. San Francisco: Jossey-Bass, 1987.

Galbraith, M. W. "Certification Would Advance Professional Practice." *Lifelong Learning: An Omnibus of Practice and Research,* 1987, *11* (2), 15, 18.

Galbraith, M. W., and Gilley, J. W. "An Examination of Professional Certification." *Lifelong Learning: An Omnibus of Practice and Research,* 1985, *9* (2), 12-15.

Galbraith, M. W., and Gilley, J. W. *Professional Certification: Implications for Adult Education and HRD.* Columbus, Ohio: ERIC Clearinghouse on Adult, Career, and Vocational Education, 1986.

Penland, P. R. "Certification of School Media Specialists." *Journal of Research and Development in Education,* 1982, *16* (1), 9-12.

BARBARA A. WHITE is director of the Office of Instructional Development, Montana State University, Bozeman.

Establishing a set of intellectual standards is essential in the process of confronting controversies.

Confronting Controversies: A Call For Action

Michael W. Galbraith, Burton R. Sisco

Diversity is one of the great strengths of the adult and continuing education field. With its multitude of providers, wide array of clientele, varying opinions about the purpose and philosophy of the field, and different forms of professional training, it is little wonder that controversies exist and little or no action toward their resolution has occurred. As we suggested in Chapter One, controversies are debatable whereas problems are solvable. To begin addressing some of the more enduring controversies in our field, we believe that adult and continuing educators, both individually and collectively, must not only identify the problems but also formulate the commensurate action strategies needed to bring about their resolution. The controversy valence model for understanding controversies, presented in Chapter One, is an initial step in wrestling with this complex agenda.

We acknowledge that many controversies are more philosophically oriented and thus difficult to deal with on an action-specific level. Examples of these issues include the starting point and purpose of adult and continuing education, where leaders of the field should come from, and whether the field should be market driven. Even if these issues remain at a philosophical level, it is our hope that the field will recognize the importance of continuing the debates on them. Conversely, there are issues that not only define a number of philosophical orientations and specific problems but also invite their resolution through specific actions. Within this framework are the issues of mandatory continuing education, codes of ethics, and professional certification. Yet, even if we work through the various steps of the controversy valence model, this does not mean that a particular issue under scrutiny will have only positive consequences for

NEW DIRECTIONS FOR ADULT AND CONTINUING EDUCATION, no. 54, Summer 1992 © Jossey-Bass Publishers

adult and continuing education; there may be negative and unintentional consequences as well. This dual-edged exposure is one of the strengths of the model.

Whether an issue is characterized as philosophical or amenable to resolution through action strategies, it is imperative that adult and continuing educators develop a set of intellectual standards that can be applied to the debate process. Although not exhaustive, we offer the following suggestions and criteria that may help adult and continuing educators think about the process of confronting controversies.

Confronting Controversial Issues

In debating as well as engaging in action strategies to bring about a conclusive stance on a controversy, we must be concerned with the associated implications for enhancement of practice within the field. Brockett (1991, p. 101) states that "until adult and continuing educators gain a greater sense of their professional identity and of the kinds of directions they would like to see the field take in the coming years and until they take action to secure these directions, we run the risk of stagnation." Therefore, the process of confronting controversies involves the need to think critically about the implications for the field and also about how this affects and contributes to reflective practice. As Osterman (1990, p. 134) suggests, reflective practice consists of "mindful consideration of one's actions." It also "involves identifying one's assumptions and feelings associated with practice, theorizing about how these assumptions and feelings are functionally or dysfunctionally associated with practice, and acting on the basis of the resulting theory of practice" (Peters, 1991, p. 89).

We stated in Chapter One that most controversies begin at the personal level and then progress into a more public forum. If that is an appropriate assumption, then various strategies and criteria can be advanced that enhance our process of confronting controversies and assist in bringing about reflective practice.

Data Collection. The process of thinking about a controversy involves the assembling of information. Data collection can be accomplished by critically reading relevant literature, informally discussing various aspects of it with professional colleagues and peers, attending debates or forums dealing with a controversy, and so on.

Critical Analysis. The process of critically analyzing data involves identification of those assumptions that guide our thoughts, values, attitudes, and needs. As we begin engaging in critical thinking, we soon discover whether the controversy is grounded in a reality that is recognized within the field of adult and continuing education.

Propositional Building. It is at this point that our personal convictions, thoughts, and assumptions are moved into a more public forum for checks on validity and reliability with others in the field. Part of the propositional building process is consideration of alternative ways of thinking about a controversy.

Theorizing. Based on the critiques and refinements suggested, the next step is to engage in theorizing about the controversy in terms of how it affects general practice as well as the implications for the field. Theorizing also helps us make connections with our own specific practice and related agendas.

Connectedness. Since adult and continuing education is characterized most often as a field of practice, it is important to attend to a controversy's relevance to and implications for practice. By attending to the criteria of connectedness and by specifically addressing the consequences of a controversy, adult and continuing educators are better able to understand not only the practice-specific consequences and connections but the contextual nature of the controversy as well.

Contextuality. The confrontation with controversy and the subsequent action occur within context-specific arenas. Consequences that are derived from examining a controversial issue must also be concerned with how they impact the various practice segments of adult and continuing education, as well as the positive or negative influences on such factors as class, ethnicity, gender, and age. An explicit expression of a controversial issue requires proponents and opponents to indicate and communicate how contextual factors influence the consequences of their action.

Ethicality. Ethical dilemmas can also arise from confronting and working through controversial issues. Acceptance of or opposition to a particular position on an issue may pose certain personal, professional, and political risks to adult and continuing educators as well as to the field, and these risks should be made public.

Conclusion

The process of confronting controversies in these challenging times should be an essential and ongoing activity for those engaged in adult and continuing education. This activity provides us with the opportunity to critically and reflectively analyze the beliefs and values on which we base our professional practices. The contributors to this volume have issued a "call for action" to those who believe that the confronting of controversies is an indispensable component of the field's future growth and development.

References

Brockett, R. G. "Planning for Professional Development." In R. G. Brockett (ed.), *Professional Development for Educators of Adults*. New Directions for Adult and Continuing Education, no. 51. San Francisco: Jossey-Bass, 1991.

Osterman, K. F. "Reflective Practice: A New Agenda for Education." *Education and Urban Society,* 1990, 22 (2), 133–152.

Peters, J. M. "Strategies for Reflective Practice." In R. G. Brockett (ed.), *Professional Development for Educators of Adults.* New Directions for Adult and Continuing Education, no. 51. San Francisco: Jossey-Bass, 1991.

MICHAEL W. GALBRAITH is associate professor of adult education and coordinator of graduate studies in adult education at Temple University, Philadelphia.

BURTON R. SISCO is associate professor of adult education and coordinator of the graduate program in adult and postsecondary education at the University of Wyoming, Laramie.

INDEX

Ordering Information

New Directions for Adult and Continuing Education is a series of paperback books that explores issues of common interest to instructors, administrators, counselors, and policy makers in a broad range of adult and continuing education settings—such as colleges and universities, extension programs, businesses, the military, prisons, libraries, and museums. Books in the series are published quarterly in fall, winter, spring, and summer and are available for purchase by subscription as well as by single copy.

Subscriptions for 1992 cost $45.00 for individuals (a savings of 20 percent over single-copy prices) and $60.00 for institutions, agencies, and libraries. Please do not send institutional checks for personal subscriptions. Standing orders are accepted.

Single copies cost $14.95 when payment accompanies order. (California, New Jersey, New York, and Washington, D.C., residents please include appropriate sales tax.) Billed orders will be charged postage and handling.

Discounts for quantity orders are available. Please write to the address below for information.

All orders must include either the name of an individual or an official purchase order number. Please submit your order as follows:
  Subscriptions: specify series and year subscription is to begin
  Single copies: include individual title code (such as CE1)

Mail all orders to:
  Jossey-Bass Publishers
  350 Sansome Street
  San Francisco, California 94104

For sales outside of the United States contact:
  Maxwell Macmillan International Publishing Group
  866 Third Avenue
  New York, New York 10022